AF869782

What's left in teacher education: Teacher education, the radical left and policy proposals

Hillcole Group Papers

The Hillcole Group is a group of Radical Left Educators, formed in 1989 with three aims:
1) To influence policy and decision making on educational matters;
2) To respond rapidly to assaults on the quality of education from the Radical Right;
3) To improve the quality of schooling and of teacher education.

As a writing group, we will be producing a continuous series of publications in pursuit of the above aims. Our first five booklets are critiques of the Radical Right and the way in which their theories and policies have affected schooling, further education and teacher education. In winter 1990 we will be developing beyond critique into a set of policy proposals in our forthcoming book *Redprint for Education*. Members of the group are Stephen Ball, Caroline Benn, Clyde Chitty, Mike Cole, Debbie Epstein, Andy Green, Dave Hill, Janet Holland, Tamara Jakubowska, Ken Jones, Rehana Minhas, and Gaby Weiner.

No. 1 *Charge of the Right Brigade: The Radical Right's attack on teacher education* Dave Hill
ISBN 1 872155 00 6

No. 2 *Equal opportunities in the new ERA*
Ann Marie Davies, Janet Holland, and Rehana Minhas
ISBN 1 872767 00 1

No. 3 *Something old, something new, something borrowed, something blue: Schooling, teacher education and the Radical Right in Britain and the USA* Dave Hill
ISBN 1 872767 05 2

No. 4 *Training turns to enterprise: Vocational education in the market place* Pat Ainley
ISBN 1 872767 10 9

No. 5 *Markets Morality and Equality in Education* Stephen Ball
ISBN 1 872767 15 X

For further information about these publications please turn to the back of this book.

What's left in teacher education: Teacher education, the radical left and policy proposals

Dave Hill

Hillcole Group Paper 6

the Tufnell Press, London

the Tufnell Press,
47 Dalmeny Road,
London, N7 0DY

Copyright © 1991 Dave Hill

All rights reserved. No part of this publication may be reproduced, stored in a retrieval system, or transmitted in any form or by any means, electronic, mechanical, photocopying, recording or otherwise, without permission in writing from the publisher.

First published 1991

British Library Cataloguing in Publication Data
A catalogue record for this book is
available from the British Library

ISBN 1-872767-20-6

Printed in England by Instant Print West One, London.

Contents

Acknowledgements

I would like to thank the following for their help in criticising and editing various drafts of this booklet. Thanks to Geoff Seale of WSIHE, Hazel Waddup, Amelia Cipriano Estrela, Mike Cole and John Clay of the Hillcole Group, Geoff Whitty at Goldsmiths College, members of the NATFHE and the NUT Teacher Education Advisory Committees and the WSIHE Research Seminar who all reacted to and critiqued various drafts. And, of course, the Hillcole Group, who did the same. In particular, many thanks to Gaby Weiner for her comments, and editing, (and trenchant criticism) of various drafts. And many thanks to Alison Twine and Sue Shannon for typing, retyping, and retyping the drafts. The opinions expressed in this booklet are mine, not those of West Sussex Institute of Higher Education and not those of the above. The responsibility is mine.

Foreword

Teacher education in England and Wales is in the spotlight. It is under ferocious, sustained and nakedly ideological assault at three inter-related levels of discourse - the radical right middlebrow and quality media (in particular the *Daily Mail* and *Mail on Sunday*), radical right ideologists, think-tanks and academics, and the current (mid-1991) Conservative education Ministerial team.

Throughout this booklet, references are made to, and quotes taken from the above three types of source each of which features in 'a discourse of derision'.[1]

The mid 1991 attacks on Culloden Primary School, initially hailed widely after its BBC TV series as a model of non-sloppy, progressive, child-centred, anti-racist, anti-sexist education (at first even by the right-wing *Daily Telegraph* and *The Times*) have been like an ideological blitzkrieg. Kenneth Clarke, the Secretary of State for Education and Science, encouraging and encouraged by the *Daily Mail* and *Mail on Sunday*, has fulminated against 'cranky' approaches to the teaching of reading, damning not only the real books method but also the 'look and say' method, in favour of the 'phonics method,'[2] a condemnation extended to the institutions of teacher education propagating such approaches. In June 1991 Clarke "went beyond anything senior ministers have said before about teaching methods" (Bates, 1991b) "...targeted trendy teaching methods, the rush to introduce comprehensives and 'sinister multiculturalism' that branded Plato and Shakespeare 'dead, white European males' and struck them from study lists. There was even a swipe at Glynis Kinnock for helping to pioneer the 'real book' teaching of reading" (Massey, 1991a).

The reading methods controversy is part of the current attack on teacher education, with Tim Eggar, one of the Junior Ministers for Education baldly announcing "That in future most teachers would be trained in schools instead of teacher training schemes[3], and with a *Daily Mail* full page article announcing that

> "Our education system is in turmoil. Nowhere is that more apparent than in the teacher training colleges — A shake-up of teacher training is now certainly at the top of the Government's manifesto pledges for the next election. Education Secretary Kenneth Clarke, who has condemned child-centred learning as 'silly', has not been idle.
>
> After the 'Sharon Shrill' affair in which Cambridge classicist Annis Garfield was denied a teacher-training place at Nene College, Northamptonshire, yet was offered an interview when she posed as a fictitious Afro-Caribbean feminist, he sacked some of the 'trendies' from the quango which validates teacher-training courses.
>
> Further, he has ordered two inquiries: the first into the quality of courses approved, and the second into the way in which teachers are trained to teach reading.
>
> It is an open secret that he is outraged by some of the courses which have been approved.
>
> Ministers are itching to break the monopoly - and power - of the teacher training colleges and will use the next election to do it. The main weapon favoured by them will be 'on the job training'."[4]

Like their National Curriculum for schools, current radical right proposals for detheorising teacher education, for replacing much of it by in-school apprenticeships or by-passing it altogether, are a gigantic ideological experiment, playing with children's schooling and futures. Presented in the name of 'standards', this is an attempt to assert ideological hegemony through the ideological state apparatuses.

It is not my purpose here to give a description and critique of the two new school-based routes into teaching (the Licensed Teacher and the Articled Teacher) schemes.[5] There are currently a number of national and localised formative evaluation schemes, and a section of this booklet, "School basing, School focusing and ITE" summarises some relevant USA experience. A number of problems arise if most, or all, teacher education is school based: overloading of schools; the cost of Articled Teacher bursaries and of a one to one ratio between mentors and articled teachers and licensed teachers; the rapidly apparent desire among articled teachers for less time in school and more time to reflect and find out about explanations and theory, following sustained time in school; and concern about the context specificity of most school-based schemes. For sections of the Left (for example this booklet), there are inherent problems as theory, critique, reflection, intellectual rigour and the skills these generate substantially disappear from teacher training. On the Right, Ministers have apparently already pre-judged in favour of such schemes (see Macleod, 1991, Massey, 1991b), as has the ***Mail on Sunday.*** [6]

I have discussed this booklet and its proposals in draft form with the Teacher Education Sub-Committees of the main Teachers' Union (the NUT), the main College Lecturers' Union (NATFHE), the Hillcole Group of Radical Left Educators, with a group of Left Teacher Educators at the Easter 1991 Bath University Conference 'Conceptualising Reflection in Teacher Development' - and also with Andrew Smith MP, Labour's spokesperson for Teacher Education. As a result, the booklet and policy proposals have been extended and modified, and such modifications will continue. The Hillcole Group are organising an invitation National Seminar on Teacher Education 'CATE, post-CATE and a National Curriculum for Initial Teacher Education - What should a Labour Government do? Perspectives from the Left' (open to the democratic Left) in July 1991, and an open International Conference on the Left and Teacher Education in March 1992.

The purpose of this booklet, and of the Seminar and Conference, is ideological. It is an attempt at a Left response to the current assault, at both polemical and at academic/theoretical levels. It attempts to go beyond defence, beyond cautious retrenchment, into attack, into Left policy-making for a Labour Government. The proposals herein are based on a belief that teachers must not only be skilled, competent, classroom technicians - but that they should be much more than that. They must also be critical, reflective, transformative and intellectual. They should themselves, and should enable and encourage their pupils/students, not only to gain basic and advanced knowledge and skills. They should enable and encourage their pupils/students to question, critique, judge and evaluate what is, what effects it has, and why. And to be concerned and informed about equality and social justice. Not just in school, but in life beyond the classroom door.

Notes to the foreword

1. A phrase used by Meg Maguire in Maguire (1991).
2. For the events surrounding and developing from Culloden Primary School in 1991 see articles in the *Mail on Sunday* and *Daily Mail* by Lightfoot (1991a,b), Gordon (1991) and Massey (1991b, c). For the Culloden version see Culloden School (1991). A scathing attack on the HMI Report on Culloden School (HMI 1991), is made by Robin Richardson (1991).
3. Lodge (1991a).
4. Massey (1991c).
5. Hill (1989a, 1990a). Jean Bocock (1991) gives a brief description and critique of "Reflections on a decade of Conservative Government 'management' of teacher education." Currently (May 1991) there are 439 Licensed Teachers employed in 44 local authorities. 290 are graduates.
6. Gordon, A. (1991) 'Teacher is the pupil in a class of her own' *Mail on Sunday*, 5 May. A glowing report included the following

> "XXX is one of the first 400 graduates to start training under the Government's controversial articled teacher scheme.
>
> The aim is to improve standards in Britain's schools with staff who are not brainwashed by trendy theories expounded in teacher-training colleges.
>
> The brave new breed of teachers are paid £5,000 a year to gain experience on the job for four days and go to college for formal instruction only one day a week.
>
> A Department of Education spokesman said: 'We are more interested in teachers being able to teach than teachers with too much theory.'"

There are three clients of the teacher education system. First, the national education service; second, teacher trainees/teacher education students , and third schools themselves - not only within England and Wales, but, post 1992, in the European Community. Institutions of teacher education - University Departments of Education, Polytechnics, Colleges/Institutes of Higher Education - are the producers, the providers, the developers of future teachers and also beneficiaries of the system.

The current debate on teacher education

There are three current debates about teacher education:- those of teacher supply, teacher retention and the teacher education curriculum - how to train/educate new teachers.

This booklet makes policy proposals for the third of these, the teacher education curriculum. It is deliberately written in two registers, the polemical/rhetorical and the academic.

It will concentrate on the following issues within teacher education:

(i) its philosophy and model of the teacher;

(ii) the balance of content between a) Main Subject, b) Professional Curriculum/Skill, c) Professional Critical/Theoretical, d) School experience;

(iii) the overall amount of school experience;

(iv) entry and exit criteria for IT (Initial Training) courses;

(v) length of courses;

(vi) the nature and extent of the relationship between schools and colleges.

A number of perspectives about teacher education/training have emerged in recent years. Since the late 1980s in particular, following the legislative and publicity attempt to 'settle' schools and teachers, the Radical Right critical spotlight has been harshly focused on teacher education.

Two current models of initial teacher education are commonly presented as alternatives to each other:

(1) the classroom competency/skills model,

(2) the reflective practitioner model.

But these are not the only models. There is a third, a 'radical left', model of the teacher which is a distinctive variant of the reflective practitioner model - distinctive in its pedagogy, in its Initial Teacher Education curriculum content and in its intention. This model, promulgated by this paper, is

(3) the critical reflective 'transformative' practitioner model.[1]

In practice longer courses such as 4-year full-time B.Ed. (Bachelor of Education degree) courses tend to and claim to attempt to develop the reflective practitioner model, whereas, many shorter courses such as the 1-year full-time PGCE (Post-Graduate Certificate in Education) decide to concentrate mainly on the competency skill model.

The PGCE course is only 36 to 37 weeks long. Approximately 14 weeks of this is commonly spent on teaching practice, leaving around 23 weeks, - 115 days - for college-based courses. Some courses spend longer in schools, whether on block teaching practice or on serial (weekly) practice or a combination of both.

The difficulties of attempting to develop in students 'reflection-in-action' or 'reflection-on-action'[2] within such a short time are widely recognised. Many course tutors and course outlines[3] do attempt to develop 'reflective practitioners', or even 'critical reflective transformative practitioners'. But how realistic is this within 115 days?

The apparent dichotomy or polarisation between the competency/skills model of the teacher on the one hand, and the reflective practitioner model should be challenged. These are not, in my view, incompatible.

Four perspectives on teacher education

Within the ideological debate there are a number of, by now quite well known, broad positions:[4] The 'Radical Right' and 'Hard Centre' tend to argue for the classroom competency/skills model, the 'Soft Centre' and the 'Left in the Centre' for the reflective practitioner model, the 'Radical Left' for the critical, reflective, transformative practitioner model.

The radical right

'Radical Right' writers on education and on teacher education in Britain include the Hillgate Group, (Roger Scruton and Caroline Cox among others), Stuart Sexton, Anthony O'Hear, Dennis O'Keefe, Rhodes Boyson, Beverley Shaw and Sheila Lawlor, supported by numerous articles in *The Times, Daily Telegraph, Daily Mail* and their Sunday versions, and *Times Educational Supplement.* Their writings include the flimsily researched Centre for Policy Studies 'Report' attacking college-based teacher education by Sheila Lawlor which was accompanied by leading articles and editorial comment in a number of right-wing daily newspapers and weeklies such as the *Times Educational Supplement,* some controlled by Rupert Murdoch[5].

Common interrelated themes of the Radical Right in respect of teacher education are that:

- the present college-based system of teacher education should be scrapped (either totally or substantially);[6]
- school based on-the-job skill development, such as the Licensed Teacher Scheme, should become the major type of teacher training;[7]
- college-based teacher education is too much concerned with changing society and/or developing egalitarian or liberal perspectives on schooling and society;[8]
- in particular, college-based teacher education promulgates a model of the multi-cultural and anti-racist teacher;[9]
- college-based teacher education concentrates too little on classroom discipline skills;[10]
- college-based teacher education is too progressive and child-centred;[11]
- other than practical skills, teachers also need "knowledge and love of the subject to be taught;"[12]
- there is no or little need for educational theory;[13]

Three centre perspectives

A view has emerged which could be described as the social democratic/liberal democratic/soft/'wet' Conservative consensus. This has been broadly in tune with professional teacher union and 'official' body opinion. This (in my view) is the perspective of much of the current 'educational establishment', with a broad set of views defending much of the educational philosophy of the 1960s and 1970s. It is moderate, progressive, child-centred and generally supports college-based teacher education developments, as updated by the 1984 and 1989 requirements of the Committee for the Accreditation of Teacher Education (CATE), and by the 1991 National Curriculum Council (NCC) document 'The National Curriculum and the Initial Training of Student, Articled and Licensed Teachers'.

Two major aspects of CATE of 1984 are the requirement that teacher education lecturers should have 'recent, relevant and substantial' teaching experience in schools; and secondly, that the 'Main Subject Study' in the B.Ed. degree be upgraded to 50% of time on the B.Ed. The major current 1989 requirement of CATE is that teacher trainers should undertake school teaching experience equivalent to one term in every five years. The 1989 document requires that institutions reach this standard by the academic year 1992-93. The NCC document, together with the CATE criteria are, in effect, a new National Curriculum for Initial Teacher Education, relating ITE to the National Curriculum for schools.[14]

Within this broadly Centrist group the three distinguishable sub-groups are the 'Soft Centre', the 'Hard Centre' and the 'Left in the Centre'.

The 'soft centre'

This group argues that 'everything in the garden is rosy', Nirvana would exist if there were more resourcing and people would 'let us get on with the job'. This is a not untypical 'producer' view, and is the view of a number of teacher education institutions and college/university department of education lecturers. Sometimes it is borne out of genuine ideological support for those 'Plowdenite', 'comprehensivist', and sometimes, 'equal opportunities' policies in schooling and education and not simply out of the innate comfort or conservatism of not wanting to change.

'The hard centre'

Another collection of individuals seek to accept some of the critique of the Radical Right. Such 'Hard-Centre' teacher educators, for example David Hargreaves and Mary Warnock,[15] do not appear to be organised into formal groupings. Among them there seems to be a consensus emerging about some of the below points. They see something wrong with the state of teacher education, and welcome the blowing away of the cobwebs, the opening up of these debates. They accept a combination of:

1. Easier academic entry qualifications onto Initial Training (IT) courses if it is tied to maturity and previous experience;
2. Shortened courses on the lines of the shortage subject shortened B.Ed. 2-year courses;
3. Other models of shortage courses (of which there are few examples in England);
4. A reduction in (effectively an attack on) reflective theory on macro- issues, radical theory and practice relating to critical theory and egalitarianism, together with an increase in time on classroom competencies and skills;
5. Virtual totally school-based siting of Initial Teacher Education (ITE) (as in the Licensed Teacher Scheme)
6. Substantially school-based siting of ITE (as in the Articled Teacher Scheme). This last view is particularly associated with David Hargreaves in a series of attacks on the B.Ed. degree in *The Times Educational Supplement*.
7. School-based siting (of the 'substantial' rather than 'total' model) either in specially selected teaching schools, (which might include City Technology Colleges), or involving a much wider use of schools, even rotating the experience to involve most or all schools.

They have recently been joined by Michael Bassey (1991) arguing for the abandonment of the four year B.Ed. and its replacement by a two year PGCE. I have no idea whether he is Left, Right or Centre, but his argument is that the four year B.Ed. is 'too complicated' and 'too demanding on staff, and that students cannot achieve high standards in professional practice'. Yet he assumes that the two years professional development in forms of two year (post-graduate) professional training will do the job better than that half (two years equivalent) of the B.Ed degree devoted to professional training.

These may well be supported not just by atavistic Radical Righters but also by some levels of college managements flexing their newly strengthened autonomous managerial muscles, delighting in shaking up existing practice and staffs.

Other college teacher educators appear to act from expediency either habitually, bending to every authoritative wind that blows, or selectively, partly on the grounds of avoiding retribution, cuts in funding or cuts in student numbers. This sub-group of the Centre is not, as far as I am aware, an identifiable organised grouping nor do they all accept all seven of the proposals. In any case some of these proposals are alternatives to each other. But they seem to accept, emphasise or demand: more school-basing, more skills/competency training, less critical theory and egalitarianism, shorter courses, and easier access into teacher education and teaching.

The 'left in the centre'

This group is comprised of individuals and networks whose ideological orientations are left of centre, sometimes a little, sometimes a lot.

Groups and initiatives have been set up by BERA (the British Education Research Association), by UCET (the Universities Council for the Education of Teachers), by 'The Future of Teacher Training' (sic) Writing Group, co-ordinated by Jean Rudduck and David Bridges, and by the 'Imaginative Projects: Arguments for a New Teacher Education' group whose publication of that name was published in January 1991.[16]

The apparent intentions and the group writings of these various groups, however left their personal politics might be, differ little from those of the 'Soft Centre'. In some cases this derives from the politics of the lowest common denominator in opposing Radical Right attacks on teacher education. In other cases it may derive from other aspects of 'reformism' - such as moderating views in the hope of gathering wider support and wider alliances. While such initiatives are welcome for those reasons implicit in political 'reformism' or 'revisionism', they do fail to go much beyond a defence of and rationale for the status quo - they neglect overt and explicit issues of social justice and equality. While individually and collectively many adherents and activists in such networks are highly committed to such issues informing initial teacher education, these concerns are not made explicit in their group activities, or if they are, instead of being neon-lit, they are in places illuminated by a flickering candle.

An example of 'Left in the Centre' writing is the booklet written by Ian Hextall, Martin Lawn, Ian Menter, Susan Sidgwick, and Stephen Walker, 'Imaginative Projects: Arguments for a New Teacher Education'. In it the writers incisively critique the Radical Right's attack on teacher education, and current developments in ITE, defining and rationalising reflective teacher education very clearly. It is a valuable document in these respects. But it offers a limited critique and programme. In thirty-five pages it avoids explicit development of a 'critical arena' of reflection - socio-political reflection. In the whole booklet there is one sentence on 'critical reflection on practice' and one of their five 'principles' (assumptions about the nature and purpose of education forming the basis of teacher education) is 'critical-theoretical'.[17]

That principle is that they 'see education as a process of empowering people with the understanding and competencies which increases effective participation in our society, and enables people to define and realise their identity, think critically about the world, and to change it'.

While this may well be a principle informing the writers' individual practice and perspectives it is difficult to see how it has informed their booklet in any explicit way. While the booklet has considerable value, it could have been written by the Soft Centre. It is too early to pass similar comments about 'The Future of Teacher Training Writing Group' convened by Jean Rudduck and David Bridges.

The highly commendable aims of that group are as follows:

'1. to defend/advance a view of: teachers as intelligent, thinking practitioners; teaching as a form of practice which has constantly to be informed by sensitivity to and intelligent reflection upon what is happening in the classroom; and teaching training as an activity which has to support and develop that sensitivity, intelligence and reflectiveness in practice.

2. to defend/advance the distinctive contribution which institutions of higher education have to make to the development of practice thus conceived (at the same time as valuing the distinctive contribution that in school practitioners can make to that training in partnership with HE).

3. to challenge and correct some of the mythology about current teacher training propagated by the 'raving right'; that current training is entirely disassociated from practical experience in schools (they seem to have no idea of the amount of time that students spend in school-based work with or without tutors); that practising teachers play no significant part in the selection, training or assessment of student teachers (they of course play a very active part in most institutions); that the curriculum of teacher training is largely determined by the ideological whims of teacher educators (they do not seem to have heard of CATE or the Secretary of State's requirements).

4. to disentangle some of the muddle about the relationship (or otherwise) between: (i) the character and quality of initial training; (ii) the recruitment and retention of teachers; (iii) the mismatch between initial training qualifications and the posts held by large numbers of teachers.

5. to demonstrate our own capacity to think and work creatively: (i) to improve the quality of initial training and develop constructive approaches to the continuing professional development of teachers; (ii) to extend

access to initial training programmes and contribute through effective programmes of professional development to the retention and career mobility of teachers; (iii) to provide appropriate career change and retraining support for teachers; (iv) to work in effective partnership with practising teachers.'

A number of the ten Polytechnic and University signatories to that manifesto can be regarded as Left of Centre in varying degrees.

However, like the Hextall/Lawn 'Imaginative Projects' group, their collaborative intentions are, in one sense, minimalist. No doubt their intention is to maximise the breadth and depth of their embrace and impact - honourable intentions - but they are not, as a group, overtly about the development of critical reflective transformative intellectuals.

In making this criticism I am well aware that many of those involved, for example, Donald McIntyre, have written forcefully about the need for student teacher to develop 'a critical understanding of the curriculum and pedagogy of their subject(s)' and an appreciation of the potentialities and the problems of achieving social justice in their own teaching.[18]

I am also aware that the group/network has hardly begun to function. But, as it stands, its five intentions, while laudable, are not Radical and are not identifiably Left. Perhaps it's effects might be.

The radical left

The fourth ideological perspective is that of the Radical Left, of which the Hillcole Group is representative. There are a variety of radical left individuals involved in teacher education, but, as yet, other than the Hillcole Group, their views have not been voiced in Radical Left form as part of an identifiable organised grouping.

The Hillcole Group holds a belief in a 'bottom-up' grassroots model of socialism rather than a monolithic 'top-down' model. The political backgrounds of the members of this group vary. In addition to holding a social class perspective they are as a group strongly influenced by the anti-racist, anti-sexist, feminist, and/or anti-homophobic grassroots activism of the Left in the 1980s. Some have been influenced by Gramsci and resistance theorists, and by USA critical theorist and teacher educators such as Giroux, McLaren, Apple and Zeichner. Others are influenced by British and West European left models from Sweden, France, West Germany and Portugal.

In several Hillcole publications current developments in teacher education are analysed in terms of ideology and the clash of cultures.[19] This paper is also written from a Radical Left perspective. It suggests that teacher education must encourage and facilitate the development of teachers who display civic courage in pursuing social justice and equal opportunities in the classroom, school and society.

The critique and proposals in this booklet differ from those of the Centre and the Radical Right. It rejects *total* school-siting/basing of ITE and also rejects *overwhelmingly* school-based ITE It rejects assaults on theory, critical reflection, social justice and egalitarianism. This paper seeks to develop a policy for teacher education which will be discussed and implemented by a Labour Government. The paper does however accept reform in ITE. But the rationale and suggested implementation of, for example, increased use of school focusing, or a national curriculum for ITE, differ from those of the Radical Right and the Centre positions. They are drawn from different ideological perspectives and have different intentions.

What initial teacher education needs: A left ideological perspective

Some differences, or differences in emphasis, between the Radical Left and the Left in the Centre concerning schooling, education, and teacher education relate to the Radical Left's:

i. emphasis on social justice *vis-à-vis* economic modernisation

ii. concept of equality as being 'egalitarian' rather than 'more efficiently meritocratic', i.e. relating to lower differentials in society rather than high or higher differentials between top and bottom in a more socially mobile meritocracy

iii. stress on the emancipatory, transformative, and critical dimensions of education and of teacher education,

iv. concern with a broader definition of 'standards' than narrowly defined and narrowly tested academic attainment

v. concern with democracy within education, schools, colleges and classrooms, in opposition to increasingly hierarchical and elitist systems of institutional and classroom management.

Initial Teacher Education should be based on:

i. Resistance to totally or overwhelmingly school-based teacher education i.e. retaining a substantial college-based role;

ii. The development of macro- and micro-theory regarding teaching and learning, in which the socio-political and economic contexts of schooling and education are made explicit;

iii. The development of effective classroom skilled teachers able to interrelate and critique theory and practice - their own and that of others;

iv. The development of teachers as critical 'transformative intellectuals' and democratic participative professionals and citizens.

The four points above reflect a particular view of the general and imprecise concept of 'the reflective practitioner'. This term, like the term 'democratic' or 'community involvement', has been open to a variety of interpretations in USA and Britain.

For example Rosaen, Roth and Lanier in their 1990 AERA paper, 'Becoming a Reflective Teacher of Subject Matter' neatly summarise Liston and Zeichman's levels, or distinct "arenas of analysis and appraisal for reflective activity, that are described in the literature on reflection."[20]

On one level, they argue, prospective teachers should reflect about the pedagogical and curricula means used to attain educational aims. Second they should examine and appraise the underlying assumptions and consequences of pedagogical action. Third they should analyse the moral implications of pedagogical actions and the structure of schooling. One way teacher educators differ is in their view of which of these "arenas" is an appropriate starting point for reflection in the learning-to-teach process. Another way teacher educators differ is the extent to which they consider the third arena, the moral/socio-political arena, should be included in the teacher education curriculum.

Three 'arenas' or types of reflection

1. Reflecting on curriculum and pedagogy

Some programmes focus very specifically on one arena of reflection: helping prospective teachers critically examine concepts related to pedagogy and curriculum as part of their professional coursework. The assumption is that by fostering critical appraisal of course concepts through reflective activity, prospective teachers will better understand the concepts they will later need in their teaching.[21]

2. Reflecting on theory and practice

Still others incorporate two arenas of reflection in the learning-to-teach process by having students examine:

(a) curriculum and pedagogy, and

(b) the consequences of pedagogical action.[22]

An attempt is made to provide a bridge between learning of theory through professional coursework and the realities of classroom life through various types of "field experiences". Reflection about consequences of pedagogical action is often facilitated by using particular strategies such as having students conduct action research, ethnographic studies and case studies accompanied by discussions, journal writing and written cases. Thus, the starting point for learning to be a "reflective teacher" is learning to analyse carefully pedagogical and curriculum issues, using program and course concepts as conceptual tools for analysis which then guide one's classroom teaching.

3. Reflecting on issues of schooling and society

Some teacher education programmes are structured to facilitate reflection in a third arena, having prospective teachers consider the moral implications of pedagogical actions and the structure of schooling as a major reflective activity.[23] Future teachers are encouraged to confront the moral dilemmas of instruction and conditions of schooling in a deliberate fashion. They are taught to examine ways in which the structure of schooling influences classroom learning (e.g. tracking, ability grouping, curriculum selection practices).[24]

In her paper to the 1990 AERA Annual Meeting, "Reflection : Out on a Limb : An Intrapersonal Process and the Development of Voice", Christine Canning describes the process of reflection resulting from the redesign of the student teaching curriculum at the University of Northern Iowa in consultation with Ken Zeichner, probably the USA's most prolific radical writer on teacher education.[25]

Although the paper refers primarily to 'arenas' of reflection 1 and 2, it is a useful addition, in its methodology, to the various examples of attempts at arena 3, i.e. those reflecting on issues of schooling and society.

This position emerges also in a number of critical Initial Teacher Education courses which are briefly set out in recent books and articles. Examples here are Clay, Cole and Hill's (1990), 'Black Under-Achievement in Initial Teacher Education', 'The Citizen as 'individual' and nationalist or 'social' and internationalist? What is the role of education?' by Cole, Clay and Hill,[26] in Mike Cole's 'Education for Equality',[27] and in Troyna and Sikes'[28] 'Putting the Why back into teacher education' in Forum, Autumn 1989, which describes the BA and QTS (Qualified Teacher Status) at Warwick University based on biographical life histories in the conviction that personal experiences and understanding provide an ideal basis from which to begin to explore why we, and others, hold particular beliefs and values and why we, and they, do things in certain ways.[29] Two other courses are set out in Hill (1989a). The then mandatory third year sixty hour B.Ed course at West Sussex Institute of Higher Education 'Schools and Society' (1988-89), and the optional 20 hour Year One and Two B.Ed courses 'Contexts for Learning' (1987-89) at Brighton Polytechnic. The PGCE course at Sheffield University attempts an innovative approach to the formation of the reflective, critical, teacher and is described in *Forum*, Spring 1989, 27.

Such courses are clear attempts to combat current anti-theoretical and anti-critical attacks on British teacher education. In Troyna and Sikes words. "Training students to be mere functionaries in our schools rather than educating them to assume a more creative and, dare we say it, critical role is precisely the name of the game at the moment. But should we abandon pre-service education courses entirely and hand the reins over entirely to practising teachers? We think not."[30]

They add, 'Research evidence suggests that many teachers continue, consciously or otherwise, to make important decisions about the organisation, orientation and delivery of the formal and informal curricula on grounds which are racist, sexist and discriminatory in a range of significant ways. Should we therefore succumb to a system of teacher education/training in which these practices could well be reproduced systematically? Or should we, instead, develop pre-service courses geared towards the development of a teaching force which reflects in a critical manner on taken-for-granted assumptions, which can articulate reasons for contesting some of the conventional wisdoms about pupils, their interests and abilities, and which, ultimately, might influence future cohorts? In short, shouldn't we be encouraging students to be intellectual about being practical?'[31]

I have tried to set out similar critiques of current developments in various places.[32] It is this critique that informs the policy proposals in this paper.[33]

The current culture clash

The current culture clash is between what might still be called, despite Mrs. Thatcher's resignation as British Prime Minister, the Thatcherite culture of privatised service and private interest culture on the one hand, against a socialist culture of public service and public interest. In the first six months since her demise, there has been no apparent let-up by the Conservative Government in the application of Radical Right competitive, individualistic, privatising, elitist, differentiating, Hayekian policies regarding schools or teacher education.

The former consensual liberal democratic culture of the 1960s and 1970s is left looking bewildered, seeking to de-ideologise education, to retreat from the culture wars and to camp out on the lowlands of pragmatism and competency training. It has retreated from egalitarianism on grounds of expediency and/or faint-heartedness.

A number of teacher educators have put their heads above the parapet in publications or the media. These include Ted Wragg, Tim Brighouse, Maurice Craft, Diane Montgomery, Peter Newsam, Jean Rudduck, Anthony Adams, Witold Tulasiewicz, and Bill Taylor, the Chair of CATE.[34] Another exception was the round robin letter signed by many University teacher educators in a scathing and effective attack on two 1990 Radical Right publications, by Sheila Lawlor and Dennis O'Keefe.[35] Various papers at the 1990 UCET Conference attacked the Radical Right onslaught on Initial Teacher Education and an April 1991 UCET Press Conference and Release further attacked misrepresentation of our work and suggested that 'the theory/practice polarisation was not an appropriate way of categorising the content of ITT courses today; the theory and the practice were fully integrated.'[36] Other exceptions are the two 'Left of Centre' groups discussed above. And a number of chapters in Booth, Furlong, and Wilkin's 1990 book, 'Partnership in Initial Teacher Training' critique current developments in teacher education ideologically, for example chapters by Margaret Wilkin, by Crozier, Mentor and Pollard, and by Wragg. So too does Robert Cowens' chapter in Norman Graves' 1990 collection, 'Initial Teacher Education: Policies and Progress.'[37]

Relationships between schools and ITE institutions

Recent developments

What should be the relationship between schools and institutions of teacher education?

The relationships between Institutions for training and schools have historically tended to involve a cycle of blame, i.e. schools blaming colleges for teachers being unprepared for the real world of the classroom, and colleges saying that students with up to date training meet old guard resistance in the staffroom. However alliances have historically and contemporaneously been built over issues of resourcing (The Education Alliance) and have combined in rejection of both the Licensed Teachers Scheme and over testing and opting out aspects of the Education Reform Act. Both groups, schools, (teachers, teacher unions) and institutions of teacher education have united to defend the dominant child-centred, liberal democratic ethos of the post-Plowden era and also some of the more radical equal opportunities developments of the late Seventies and late Eighties, in particular anti-sexism and anti-racism. This is particularly true of the National Union of Teachers.

The 'taken for granted' relationship between schools and institutions of teacher education typical of the 1970s and 1980s has been split asunder by:

- The imposition of the National Curriculum onto the schools with accompanying statutory testing and its implications for Initial Teaching Education.
- The introduction and evaluation of teacher education courses with more school based involvement, supported by CATE (though in a fairly modest way), trumpeted by radical right wing think tanks and media, and adopted as a model by growing numbers of ITE academics from Right to Left.
- Heads taking over a training role in their own institutions, and heads and senior teachers making a bigger contribution to college courses and in-service training.
- School staff and LEA staff being more involved in the planning and evaluation of courses as recommended by the 1989 CATE criteria.
- The need for college tutors to have more 'recent, relevant and substantial' teaching experience in schools.

- The need for shorter courses, and courses with different access and exit levels because of teacher recruitment and retention problems.
- In short, alongside the current Radical Right attacks on schooling standards and on teachers there has been a series of developments seeking to render ITE less isolated from schools and to increase school teacher involvement in ITE and ITE lecturing staff involvement in schools.

This suggests a new combined role for schools and colleges, with crossing of professional boundaries, and a willingness to examine strengths and weaknesses to the mutual benefit of both institution and the students.

What do schools want?

There are many examples in various forms of schools' responses to the products of ITE, to probationer teachers.

In a major survey of 297 probationer teachers the British Inspectors of Education (the HMI) Document used a tripartite methodology. The HMI observed how the new teachers teach, they interviewed students for their views on how well they felt they had been prepared by the teacher training/ education, and thirdly they interviewed school teachers concerned with helping and advising probationers.

The HMI investigation published in 1988 on 'The New Teacher in School'[38] highlighted areas in which newly 297 qualified teachers felt inadequately prepared by their ITE courses. Although it was carried out on students whose courses were unaffected by the CATE 1984[39] criteria it did itemise, in valuable detail, a number of competencies and probationer teachers' evaluations of those competencies and areas of awareness.

In a smaller scale, unpublished study of forty teachers, headteachers and advisory teachers, Waddup and Hill looked at some of the needs voiced by these 'clients'. The study identified headteachers, teachers, and advisory teachers as clients of the education system.[40]

Sample teachers' perspectives from the Waddup and Hill survey are included in the following quotes.[41] These are representative quotes, which are not only voiced and felt needs but are understandable and admissible - needs which should be met by institutions of teacher education:

> "we need teachers who are going to stay more than one year and not want to go travelling at the end of the probationary year";
> "we need teachers and students who are up to date with the changes and the National Curriculum, as our staff are already trained and we do not want to keep back-tracking"

"we need infant staff who know the three core subjects really well, this is more important than having a specialist subject"
"we need the current debate on reading, standards, to be taken seriously, with trainees being given a thorough grounding in all the skill areas as well as the theory"
"we need more teachers with another language at junior level"
"we need teachers able to problem-solve well, and to relate theory to daily practice"
"we need assessment taught alongside all the curriculum subjects and not as a separate item"
"we need students to have an understanding of comparative systems of education"
"we need teachers to have a good knowledge of special needs because of integration"
"we need students to work alongside a teacher or tutor in a proper team teaching situation, planning and evaluating together individual lessons and activities"
"we believe tutors and senior teachers must have a better respect for each other and learn to work together as a team"
"we need teachers who understand how children's race, gender, and social background affect their learning and also affects how they are treated by teachers. "
"It is not helpful to have teachers who have become very passive and too dependent on the institution, they have difficulty in adjusting to staffroom and to school life"
"Counselling basics and work with adults is a vital part of training, also the teacher as manager of non-teaching staff"

Half of these most common responses relate (as might be expected since the Education Reform Act) to the debate with ITE about the content of ITE courses. Approximately half also relate to the nature and extent of the relationship between schools and colleges. And, importantly, around a half (there is some overlap) of the responses also relate to the debate concerning the philosophy and model of the teacher.

It appears from this study that some schools want teachers not merely to have appropriate skills, knowledge and attitudes, but to be reflective practitioners, and active, critical, reflective practitioners.

School basing, school focusing and ITE

A number of USA studies in 1990 highlighted considerable deficiencies in school-based teacher education. These included unsatisfactory provision and mentoring of student teachers in terms of their (i) observation of teaching, (ii) pre-teaching discussions, (iii) post-teaching critique and (iv) student teacher contact with and support from the classroom teacher mentor, the school support team, the local authority 'providers', (and, where they are involved, college teacher educators).[42] Will Britain's Articled and Licensed teachers and even college-based teacher trainees in the nineties suffer similar deficiencies?

A major implication of Wale and Irons' United States' study, for example, is that "mentor training needs to be expanded so that supervision becomes more than "adequate" and that it include, in addition to clinical supervision, developing communication and conferencing skills."[43] (A conclusion also of the detailed ethnographic study about the absence of a model of mentoring presented at AERA, in 1990 by Michelle Parker).[44] Recent United States' research has many lessons for the current British systems of initial teacher training - in particular for the two new school based innovations in England and Wales (the one-year Licensed Teacher scheme which started in 1989 and the two-year Articled Teacher scheme which started its mentor training in Summer 1990 and its student teaching/teacher education course in September 1990). It also has implications for partially school-based schemes such as the WSIHE Crawley B.Ed. degree, the Sussex University PGCE, the Oxford Polytechnic PGCE, the now defunct school based East Anglia PGCE, and a variety of schemes yet to be developed.

The question does arise however, that however wonderful, well-paid, well trained, well-resourced, beautifully collaborative, diligent and committed mentors are, predominantly or totally school based schemes of initial teacher education are defective. They are defective and inadequate because by their very nature. Such schemes are likely to lack:

1. Theoretical inputs;

2. Non-school based student collaborative reflective discussions. Without adequate time for both of these, student teachers, articled and licensed teachers may become in effect second class teachers, being treated in Maclennan and Seadon's terms, as 'beginner teachers' rather than 'learner teachers'.[45]

The reflectiveness discussed at AERA in 1990 by Rosaen, Roth and Lanier, and by Canning[46] among others, and, more importantly, critical reflectiveness is likely to be diminished, demeaned, and disregarded. That is, of course, subject to teacher, mentor, new teacher, teacher union, and teacher educator resistance. If such critical reflectiveness is suppressed, that will be another triumph for the ideology of Thatcherism/Reaganism.

Most vitally, such detheorising, school-based, narrow skill competency based developments in initial teacher education are subject to the policy reviews and initiatives of an incoming Labour Government. How much of current Conservative teacher education policy will the Labour Party accept and maintain? And what will it charge? What opportunities for equality and quality will it seize and develop?

The next section will deal with developments in Labour Party policy, setting out sixteen proposals for a Labour Government.

Sixteen policy proposals for teacher education

The Labour Party has recently produced two policy documents specifically on education - 'Children First' in 1989 and 'Aiming High - Raising standards in Britain's schools' in December 1990.

'Children First' contains a number of proposals for teacher education (which it unfortunately calls 'teacher training').[47]

The second, briefer document includes two paragraphs specifically on what it again calls 'teacher training':

> "Labour will introduce a national core curriculum for teacher training. Training institutions will not only certify that teachers are competent to teach, but will also provide a profile of students' strengths and weaknesses as a foundation for support and supervision during their first years in the professions".
>
> "We will set up teacher training schools. At present most of the initial, on-the-job training takes place in those schools with the largest number of vacancies and highest turnover - precisely the schools where pressures on the rest of the teaching staff make them likely to be under the greatest stress."[48]

This section of will set out ten policy proposals which Labour should implement. The first six of these proposals are a commentary on and a critical expansion of the 1989 Labour proposals. Labour's 1990 proposals for 'a national core curriculum for teacher training, for profiling students strengths and weaknesses, for supporting new teachers during their first years in the profession, and for 'teacher training schools', are commented on, respectively, in this booklet's proposals 2, 3, 1, and 6.

1. Continuing teacher education beyond initial qualification

The suggestion that the "system of Initial Teacher Training must be recast, and must cover not only the period of college-based training, but the first five years of service,"[49] is necessary though I am not convinced about the necessity for a five year period. The concern with the new teachers' 'abrupt induction' into full-time teaching, with little of a settling-in or induction period for novice teachers, is of considerable importance. It is also a central concern of recent USA papers and articles.[50] However it is important not to relegate initial teacher education to deal with practical skills and leave post-qualification, or in-service training to develop theory, as suggested in general by the Radical Right. Nor must it, exclude the 'critical/social/ideological' arena of reflection from college-based critical Teacher Education.

There are a number of reasons for opposing such a development. It would, in effect, separate practice from theory, training in classroom skills from educating student teachers to reflect on their own and others actions in schools.

One reason for opposing the 'skills first, theory and reflection afterwards' approach is that for many teachers afterwards post-qualification In-Service education never arrives.

There is a major danger that Labour will succumb to the proposal for skills based initial teacher education followed by 'reflective' in-service education.

Many teachers escape from in-service education. Reflective or critical reflective theory based courses might have only a minority recruitment among teachers. Furthermore an assumption that INSET (In-Service education for teachers) is reflective, is not necessarily the case. Much INSET is skills based and essentially non-reflective i.e., it is 'how to', rather than 'why to or why not to'.[51]

Another reason is that teachers should be reflective and critically reflective from day one of their teaching, and indeed on their teaching practices and school experience. Reflection and reflecting should inform the whole of their development as teachers and as intellectuals, with theory and practice critically informing each other.

A third reason is that induction into reflection and critical reflection is better achieved as a process, a long-term process during initial teacher education, advanced by discussion as 'learner teachers' rather than 'beginner teachers' caught up in daily, grinding, frenetic day-to-day fully timetabled teaching.[52]

In the light of the immense, and unique responsibilities placed upon newly qualified teachers, and, outside the ILEA, and the virtual collapse of induction and probationer programmes, Labour's 1989 proposal for "say 12 weeks off-school training, based upon their training institution, within their first five years" is welcome. Whether 12 weeks is enough, and whether it is feasible to base this upon training institutions needs discussing. It would certainly facilitate college evaluation of their own B.Ed. and PGCE courses. But it is probably better achieved as part of a funded probationer and new teacher in-service support programme extending the best of current practice. A related recommendation concerns the fragmentation of career development in teaching, in which, to quote Hextall et al. (1991) "validation and certification at various stages and phases of career development are currently very fragmented, incoherent and lacking in progression and direction. Hextall et al., in their *Imaginative Projects' booklet*, note that

> "No modern industry or service in Britain treats the training and education process as reducible to a short entry period. In recent years the need to produce quality goods which are reliable and effective has meant that in-house training programmes, open learning units, management consultancies, and other developmental programmes have flourished in the business world. They have done so because it is recognised that only skilled, educated employees produce high value products, and that changes in the market mean that new skills or qualities in the work force are always a basic requirement. The HMI Report, *Perspectives on Teacher Education: Other trainers views*, highlights the deficiencies in the current pattern of staff development in education when compared to the training models found in some other professional areas. We endorse a developmental model of teacher education which aims to produce a quality profession which recruits and retains staff. We do not believe that this should be based on untested claims for new training routes or new training institutions."[53]

1.1 Recommendation

There should be a nationally recognised, coherent and co-ordinated pattern of and certification for teachers' career development, incorporating initial training, induction, required INSET and additional INSET.

2. Core Curriculum for Initial Teacher Education

Much of this section of this booklet concerns what new teachers should know about, what skills they should possess, and what dispositions they should exhibit. There is value in 'letting a hundred flowers bloom', in some heterogeneity between different courses of initial teacher education, in school staffs having a complementarity of areas of knowledge, in maintaining diversity as a stimulus to innovation and experiment. There is legitimate concern, however, that some courses are not sufficiently critically reflective, not sufficiently school focused with too little time in schools, and do not develop classroom skills sufficiently. Everything in the garden is not rosy, although the blooms are brighter following implementation of the CATE 1984 and 1989 criteria. But there is a wide difference between the fertilising suggested here and the indiscriminate spraying of Radical Right 'weedkiller' or 'college and theory killer' which would stunt the whole garden.

The 1991 National Curriculum Council guidelines *The National Curriculum and the Initial Training of Student, Articled and Licensed*

Teachers gives considerable and in depth direction to ITE. It gives, in effect, 28 objectives to be met by ITT (Initial Teacher Training) courses, within the seven areas of awareness, knowledge, skills and understanding and ability listed in note 14.

The NCC in effect demands that "during their initial training, student articled and licensed teachers should, as an essential part of their wider professional training, develop (this/these) knowledge, understanding and skills." In combination with the Accreditation criteria for Initial Teacher Training Courses, set out in CATE Circular 24/89, this may now be regarded as the current National Curriculum for Initial Teacher Education.

As they read, in bald print, such combined requirements could be interpreted in ITE courses totally non-critically. The focus on the statutory framework, subject content and teaching method, assessment, recording and reporting achievement, curriculum continuity, Information Technology capability, curriculum planning and review, are leavened minimally by the requirement that newly trained teachers will need to have a view of the whole curriculum, including cross-curricular elements (dimensions, skills and themes).

If the National Curriculum for ITE is to be led by, indeed overwhelmed by and controlled by the National Curriculum for Schools, then it will be subject to the same criticisms - of being too little concerned with social implications (of science, of geography, for example or, in ITE, of education) too little concerned with issues of equality, social justice and humanity; too little concerned with societal, socio-political analysis and questioning - in short too little concerned with macro, or micro societal critique. Instead the Conservative National Curriculum is too much concerned with delivering, assessing and reproducing a National Curriculum vetted, selected, and steamrollered through by Conservative Ministers of Education, who have visibly, unapologetically and nakedly enforced their own ideological whims on the nation's children. In short, while the NCC document has a number of laudable characteristics, its underlying political aim is clear - it is ideological - intended to produce a nation of Thatcherites.

2.1 Recommendation

Labour's discussion proposal for a national core curriculum for 'teacher training' should be discussed with representative bodies including teacher and teacher educator trade unions, and bodies such as CATE and NCC, which themselves should be remodelled to include a degree of professional and trade union representation. Such discussions should be related to a reformulation of both the outline of the National Curriculum and the Programmes of Study. It should be informed by the policy proposals in this paper, by the voices of teachers, and by distinctive critical reflective content and pedagogy. It should contain not only school experience, subject studies, professional studies (teaching skills, management skills, how to teach subjects) but also wider critical reflective concerns of what schooling and education are for, what they should be like, and whose interests they do or should serve.

3. Profiling of teacher education students

The question of a profile of students' strengths and weaknesses might become acceptable but only after looking at what profile is proposed.

The HMI 'New Teacher in School' checklist is somewhat restricted and technicist in nature as an embryonic profile, and various USA profiles are even more technicist. But the use of a profile during initial teacher education and continuing during a funded induction period of some years, makes sense. This should be as part of a mutually agreed staff development programme. Such profiles are being developed on a number of ITE courses.[54] There are a number of examples in existence which have tried to take on board criticisms of the behaviourist 'tick in the box' observable performance method of profiling.

3.1 Recommendation

Profiling of student teacher achievement should be developed, but should refer not only to skills, knowledge and attitudes, but also to student teacher reflectiveness. This should include not just the ability to analyse and evaluate within a classroom and school context, but also within a societal context. And in addition to the 'ability' to analyse and evaluate, student teacher records of achievement should include the willingness to do so.

4. More school teaching practice within the context of a college-based course.

The present amount of time spent in schools on most B.Ed. and PGCE courses is ludicrously brief, as set out in section one of this paper. Commonly the equivalent of 14 or so weeks out of a course time of 36 or 37 weeks on PGCE courses is spent in schools. And on B.Ed. courses around 20 weeks or equivalent is spent in school out of a 132 week course. The problem is, if more teaching practice gets added to ITE courses, what gets taken out? The next proposal seeks to suggest an answer to this problem.

There is nothing intrinsically wrong with the Labour Party proposal to set up B.Ed three year and one term with say, the final year including a 40 week teaching practice.[55] However, bearing in mind MacLennan and

Seadon's comments[56] and the need for time and space for student group reflection, pain and laughter, such teaching practice should include regular weekly time off for such purposes. For example, students could meet every Friday afternoon during teaching practice for mutually supportive and evaluative group small group discussion.

There are a variety of models for increasing block and serial school experience. Such models as those of Oxford University, Sussex University and the University of East Anglia have received a degree of publicity and there are other courses which are innovative in this respect. Such courses include the early years B.Ed at Brighton Polytechnic, the WSIHE Crawley B.Ed. and ITE courses at Thames Polytechnic.

4.1 Recommendation

Whatever models of teaching practice/school experience are used, ITE courses should become substantially more school-focused, with students spending more time in schools.

5. Mentoring and triangularity of co-operation between schools, colleges and students

Courses of ITE should become more school based. One model here might be the Crawley B.Ed. in which a percentage (.25 to .5) of most education/ professional courses is school based. Students are to spend around 80 days in school in addition to their block teaching practices of 18 weeks. Some of these block practices could also be lengthened.

There would be some benefit in adopting the Labour Party suggestion that "new teachers should be supervised in school by designated teacher tutors, who would be rewarded for this responsibility."[57] This has certainly been a source of angst and concern during various Summer 1990 Articled Teacher Mentor Training programmes in England which I have investigated.[58] Not only must the school mentors be rewarded (one mentor's comment "I am doing this for the money" possibly reflects one major mentor consideration), but teacher educator professional tutors must also have their (partly vacation-time) commitment rewarded too. Otherwise some will not attend the mentor training sessions. And bang goes the triangularity of the college-school-student enterprise.

Supervision of students needs to be a triangular enterprise involving a partnership between college/university tutors, teachers and students. Triangularity is a well-established and fundamental feature of IT-INSET (Initial Training - In-Service Education for Teachers) components of many B.Ed. and PGCE courses involving the working together in a classroom of a class-teacher, a college tutor, and a group of around six or seven students on a regular basis over a period of time. Planning, observation and evaluation are carried out jointly in post-session teams. IT-INSET is one of the best extant examples of triangularity in British teacher education.

Teacher 'mentors' or 'teacher-co-operators', in both pre-service and post-qualification modes, need reward and time and training to enable 'high-intensity' mentoring to take place. In a number of ITE courses 'teacher co-operators' are being offered a combination of cash and certification.[59]

In order for schools to play a far more active role in the management, development, teaching, and mentoring of student teachers, school mentors need to be compensated in terms of certification, honoraria or supply cover time off school and by mentor training, and support groups.

Clearly, there is an urgent need to establish the complementary roles of school teachers and college lecturers. While such roles can be developed, college lecturers and school teachers should not spend inordinate time doing what the other can do better. School teachers are better (in McIntyre's words) at 'craft knowledge' and ITT institutions better at 'theory'. Both partners need to relate their speciality to the other, but each ultimately has her/his speciality.

The rationale for this can be found in the widespread inadequacies reported in the USA mentor teacher schemes,[60] and reactions by schools to a variety of British mentor based or 'teacher-co-operator' based developments.

5.1 Recommendation

School mentors should be paid, trained and certificated.

6. Use of client schools as 'teacher education/professional development schools'

The Labour proposal that 'teacher training schools would be established'[61] has some advantages. Certainly a number of courses already build a very close relationship with a small number of schools rather than a loose relationship with a large number of schools, involving headteachers and whole or substantial parts of school staffs in Initial Teacher Training.[62] Various papers referred to above[63] discuss the need for closer co-operation, for support from principals/heads in the development of courses. On a number of courses Headteachers and 'teacher co-operators' are involved in course development, prior to as well as after validation, course management, interviewing of students, and it is desirable for 'teacher co-operators' to have regular meetings as a team with the appropriate team of tutors. Indeed many of these developments stem from the 1989 requirements of CATE, the Committee for Accreditation of Teacher Education.

Labour's suggestion of rotating the benefits of teacher training schools seems sensible too, 'Teacher Training Schools' could become elitist. If they were to monopolise student teachers, such students might be denied to the unfavoured schools over a long period, who would thereby miss out on various benefits of being involved in the in-service development that should and can go with the professional role of co-operating in the development of entrants to the profession.

6.1 Recommendation

Schools should be designated Teacher Education Schools/Professional Development Schools both for the in-service development of those schools and for the effective preparation and education of student teachers. Such schools should be designated on a rotating basis.

6.2 Recommendation

There should also be a continuous negotiated debate and partnership between schools and institutions of ITE with for example the CATE criteria of 1989 being actually implemented in practice and not just in claims.

7. Teacher assistants, entry and exit levels for ITE courses

The call by the Labour Party (1989) for "a proper structure for teacher assistants" and for "the qualifications and experience of teachers' assistants to be fairly reflected as credits towards a teacher qualification"[64] are both welcome. The quality, experience and insights gained by many of the mature entrants to B.Ed. courses that I have interviewed (and taught) in the last few years is sometimes staggering. The Labour policy document suggests that "while we are firmly of the opinion that teaching should be an all-graduate profession - that there should be one exit level from training, there should be different entry levels."[65]

This has to be welcomed, but cautiously. The Licensed Teacher scheme and the Radical Right have advanced similar arguments. Exit levels and exit competency profiles need to be more than merely technicist. Moreover, some pre-course school experience/field experience may have an admirable quantitative dimension but not necessarily as admirable a qualitative dimension. And so it is necessary for Labour "to discuss with" (various bodies including) "the training institutions, how this greater flexibility might be achieved."[66] This could involve giving credit for evaluated pre-course field or allied field experience, and possibly involving a substantial - I would suggest no more than four days a week - teaching experience for some terms in some years, particularly in the final year of the B.Ed. degree. But in the role of 'learner teachers' rather than 'beginner teachers.'[67]

There should be easier entry in ITE for potential recruits with suitable APEL (Alternative Prior Experience and Learning) on the model of the Mature Entry Scheme already in operation in a number of Institutions of ITE. Examples are the Mature Entry Scheme to the WSIHE B.Ed. and B.A. courses, and to undergraduate courses at some of the London Polytechnics such as PNL, Thames Polytechnic, South Bank Polytechnic.

7.1 Recommendation

Teaching should remain an all-graduate profession.

7.2 Recommendation

Access to Teacher Education should be widened by a more substantial adoption by ITE institutions of APEL (Assessment of Prior Experience and Learning) procedures, and such experience as Teacher Assistants should be valued and positively assessed.

7.3 Recommendation

There should be sub-degree level certification for teacher assistants.

8. Shortened Courses

Short two-year B.Ed. courses should be established for all subjects of the Primary Curriculum and Secondary Curriculum but strictly related to point (1) above. This is not meant to imply an abandonment of four year degrees, nor to open the door (*a la* Licensed Teachers Scheme) to clapped out executives who fancy, or are pushed into, a change. It recognises instead that for some groups of professional workers trained/educated in human relations such as sub-degree level social workers or ESL assistants, and suitably certificated teacher assistants, there needs to be a course between the existing 1-year and 4-year in length.

A number of higher education institutions already give credit exemption for previous experience. With credit accumulation degrees students with appropriate prior learning and experience can be and are given accelerated progress through degrees in some institutions, but this has not yet become a systematic practice. The proposal for a 2 year B.Ed is a proposal separate from the above individualised practice of individuals proceeding through four year B.Eds. at an accelerated rate.

This should not however be a quick fix or a short cut to a sexist over-loading of primary schools with under trained, under-educated women, induced or compelled to enter the labour market. Such recruits, indeed all recruits, need high quality teacher education, unless English/Welsh teachers are to be regarded as second rate in Europe after 1992, unqualified to teach for example in Germany or France.

It would be ironic if, because of developments in total or overwhelmingly school based initial teacher education, and because of shortening of B.Ed. courses on a wide scale, newly trained school teachers were to become the educational pariahs of Western Europe. There is a danger that newly trained school teachers might be regarded as underqualified to teach in Germany or France, qualified only to take jobs as teachers' assistants. In Portugal there has been deliberate government policy to switch from school-based teacher education to college-based teacher education. One of the acknowledged reasons is to raise the quality of new Portuguese teachers to meet European Community standards.[68]

Research carried out by Hazel Waddup has highlighted concern in Germany that some of the current changes in initial teacher education - such as shortened courses - might render some English/Welsh students ineligible to teach there.

8.1 Recommendation

There should be an expansion of shortened and part-time B.Ed courses. Recognising the limited time within shortened courses available for a full 'over a period of time' development of a critical reflective teacher.

8.2 Recommendation

There should be post-entry requirement for in-service education for shortened course teachers, of one year of in-service development within the first five years of teaching.

9. Longer PGCE school-focused/based courses

On Articled Teacher courses there has been concern among teacher educators, school mentors, class teachers, and articlees themselves about the need for more college-based input (in particular on non-curriculum and non-management issues) for example on the social contexts of schooling. There have been calls for more opportunity for critical collaborative reflection and evaluation in a non-threatening environment. This is a form of resistance to the skills-based uncritical model of the teacher advanced by the 'Radical Right'.

On existing one year PGCE courses, such is the shortage of time in a 36 or 37 week course, that students in general do not have enough space or time to cope with the pain, laughter, and blitzkrieg effect of their school practice. They lack the necessary luxury of time both for collaborative and sympathetic recuperation and for systematic reflective collaborative evaluation over a period of time.

9.1 Recommendation

PGCE courses should become two-year courses on the model of the Articled Teacher, with students, as 'learner-teachers', being paid as on the present non-means tested bursary system for their two years. This is similar, in terms of payment, to the current (West) German model of teacher education. However instead of the course being 80% in school and 20% in college the ratio should be more like 3 days a week in schools for two years and two days a week in college i.e. 60/40% or 65/35%.

10. Critical Reflective Teachers

Teacher education must be concerned with and attempt to encourage the development of teachers as effective classroom practitioners who are, at the same time, 'critical reflective teachers' and 'transformative intellectuals'.[69] Among the implications of these phrases are that these teachers should be capable of, and willing, to blow peoples' minds - their own, their pupils', their colleagues' - to open up choices, alternative histories, presents and futures, to develop in themselves and in others, democratic, and critical citizenship and action both in the micro- societies of the classroom, staffroom, school, and teacher union branch, and in the wider society.

These are bold, and yet not novel, intentions. They are important at this juncture of British and Western capitalist economic, political and ideological development. At the ideological level, the Thatcher-Reagan triumphalist economic-market/morally-authoritarian, vituperatively anti- egalitarian attack on teacher education has witnessed legislation and rhetoric which seek to 'conform', to bring into line, to 'thought- control', to repress alternative visions, to ideologise more effectively the schooling and teacher education parts of the state apparatus. Their attempt is to detheorise, de-critique, and destroy current teacher education, and to replace it with skills based, national curriculum and assessment led, conservative re-formulated, uncritical teacher training.

Teachers have a duty, and should be educated into seeing their task not simply as fitting children into largely predetermined roles in the labour market, or slotting them into uncritical quiescent acceptance of Thatcherite immoral market barbarism. Thatcherism creates and feeds on envy, consumerism, selfishness, loutishness, 'loadsamoney', 'tread on your neighbour mentality', glorifying an elite while intensifying divisions in society. Children need to be able to critique existing society, to discuss and design alternative futures for themselves and their societies.

The 'Radical Right' wishes to take teacher education out of colleges and submerge trainee teachers in the rush of classroom survival with no time to reflect on and evaluate more socially valid and concerned visions of schooling and education. And the 'Hard Centre' is willing to go along with many of their proposals.

But all children should be taught to think for themselves, to evaluate, to reflect, to critique - not just the ruling elite. If trainee teachers become apprentices, learning, like butchers, on the job - they will know their dead meat and they will know how to cut it. One dead sheep is pretty much like another. But children are alive. Teachers need more than subject knowledge and classroom skills. They need to reflect on the why and why not, the individual and group similarities and differences and needs. One child can be very different from another and so can its life chances and experience of schooling - and what it needs from its teachers.

Teacher, teacher educators and parents must resist narrow restrictive and restricted competency and skills based teacher training. And insist on and develop critical reflective teachers and society.

10.1 Recommendation

All courses should retain a substantial college based element to facilitate the induction over a period of time into professional ethos, concern, awareness, and to enable students to develop reflectively as reflective evaluative and critical practitioners.

These are fourteen policy recommendations for initial teacher education. In addition there is the necessity of resourcing, and establishing a single forum for education.

11. Adequate funding for Teacher Education

It is absolutely ludicrous that, at a time of a major shortage of teachers, institutions of teacher education in the Polytechnics and Colleges sector are being penalised financially for recruiting above PCFC[70] target figures in Summer 1990. This has the effect that students teachers recruited 'above target' in September 1990 are being under-funded, that is to say, Polytechnics and Colleges are receiving hundreds of pounds less income per 'over target' student. As recognised by the Committee of Directors of Polytechnics, the unit of resource per student has deteriorated seriously in the last two years. As recognised by NATFHE they have deteriorated even more seriously since 1979, with student/staff ratios almost twice as high over that period

11.1 Recommendation

There should be funding for enough student teachers to meet the current teacher shortage.

12. Establishing an Advisory Council for Teacher Education

At present there is no single forum for teacher education. There are many (the same applies to teaching). UCET, SCETT, NATFHE, AUT, school teacher unions, and many other representative bodies each make their own voices heard, but there is no structured standing group for teacher education at which all relevant bodies can consider the content, structure and focus of delivery of ITE courses, as noted by Bill Taylor, CATE's chair.[72]

12.1 Recommendation

A representative Advisory Council for Teacher Education should be established.

Conclusion

As a conclusion to this discussion teacher educators, and the Labour Education Team must not get swept along in a reactionary Victorian value tidal wave emulating Conservative policy willy-nilly.

The emancipatory, critical, and transformatory role of educators and of education and schooling must not be submerged by the twin waves of concern over teacher shortage and over 'practical skills'.

While accepting that the school-based element of current English B.Ed and PGCE courses should be increased, teachers, teacher educators, and political decision makers such as Jack Straw should resist current attempts to take the theory out of teacher education, take the critical thinking out of teachers minds, and take teacher education wholesale out of colleges.

Notes

1. This model is particularly associated with the work of Henry Giroux such as: Giroux & McLaren (1989); Aronowitz & Giroux (1986); and Giroux (1989). See also Hill (1989a) and Liston & Zeichner (1990).

The competency/skills model of the teacher is related to the attempt to proletarianise the teaching force. In Britain teaching is becoming de-skilled, intensified, underpaid, demotivated, militant, and a short-stay occupation. Current changes in schooling and the role and tasks of teachers (the imposition of the new National Curriculum and its compulsory standardised assessment of pupils at the ages of 7, 11, 14 and 16) can be analysed as deskilling teachers, boxing them in by a more predetermined curriculum, with teachers being appraised (and, ultimately, possibly paid) for attaining productivity assessment targets. Teachers will fall under a new form of check-list management and bureaucratic control, closer supervision. Teachers are already becoming more like supervisors of a predetermined classroom production process. Their job will be to keep students 'on task', disciplining those who disrupt the production process, and keeping track of production records - primarily through administering and recording standardized test data. (See Carlson 1988; 1990)

Part of the deprofessionalising of teachers is the separation of policy in schools from its execution, and the increased pay and power differentiation between managers and the managed, between Headteachers and teachers. Increasingly policy will be handed down by the management team, to be carried out by the teacher-technicians. The introduction of teacher contracts with greater definition of tasks and hours is directly related to the shift from professional to technical labour. Teachers, with new contracts, the National Curriculum and compulsory competitive assessment, are less and less in a position to make their own priorities and autonomous judgements. Not only is teaching becoming deskilled it is becoming, as a job, more intensified. GCSE marking, more frequent assessments and hours of recording results makes teaching 'life on the run', scarcely pausing for coffee, reflection, or study.

The third aspect of proletarianisation is reflected in teachers' pay - teaching becomes an unprized profession not only in the rhetoric of media 'knocking copy', but in the monthly salary cheque.

In these three aspects teachers are being constructed as a type of technical labourer. A fourth aspect is teacher militancy and resistance, as expressed in the unprecedented 'teacher action' of the late 1980s, continuing incidentally in the Easter 1989 NUT Conference with its substantial calls for strike action against the introduction of licensed teachers in any school. (See Hill, 1989). For Portuguese analysis of such developments see Silva (1990) and Teodoro (1990).

2. These concepts are from Schon (1983; 1989). They have been further discussed in McIntyre (1990), Blake and Blake (1990).

3. Such claims are made for a number of PGCE courses such as those at Oxford Polytechnic and West Sussex Institute of Higher Education.

A number of recent books detail and discuss developments and their ideologies in

British initial teacher education, such as Whitty, Barton, and Pollard (1987), Booth, Furlong and Wilkin (1990), and Graves (ed.) (1990). The Licensed and Articled Teacher Schemes are set out and/or described in DES (1989a, 1989e, 1989f, and 1989g).

4. This ideological debate and culture war is discussed in Hill (1989a, 1990a) drawing on Giroux, McLaren, Apple, Liston, Zeichner, and Portuguese studies by Stoer and Fernandes. In the USA it has been critiqued in Apple (1989a, 1989b) and Giroux.

5. Lawlor (1990a, 1990b). The Radical Right in Britain have been influenced in particular by the philosophy of Friedrich von Hayek with its emphasis on individual choice, competition, inequality, and neo-liberal economic policies, and by the monetarism of Milton Friedman. They have heavily influenced the policy of the Thatcher Government in Britain (1979-90) through the use of 'think tanks' such as the Centre for Policy Studies, the Adam Smith Institute, the Social Affairs Unit, and the Hillgate Group. This last group restricts itself to educational matters. There have been many books and articles describing, analysing, and critiquing the effect of Thatcherism and the Radical Right on education. See for example Hessari and Hill (1989), Chitty (1989), Jones (1989), and Hillcole Group (1991 in press). The influence of Hayek on Radical Right thinking in Britain and the 1988 Education Reform Act are set out in Ball (1990), and Wragg (1988). From a radical right perspective and analysis of the Radical Right and Education in Britain, see Knight (1990). A summary of the influence of the Radical Right and the conflict within that perspective between the authoritarian Right and the neo-Liberal right is contained in the *Times Educational Supplement* (1989).

6. The Hillgate Group (1989); Sexton (1987); Lawlor (1990); Trend (1988); Boyson (1990); O'Hear (1991).

7. Idem.

8. Shaw (1987); O'Hear (1988, 1990); the Hillgate Group (1986); O'Keefe (1990a, 1990b).

9. O'Hear (1988); the Hillgate Group (1986, 1987) and Shaw (1987). It is noticeable that while the right-wing press in Britain pillories social class egalitarianism ('anti-classism'), anti-racism, anti-sexism, and anti-heterosexism consistently, there is less emphasis on anti-anti-sexism in the writings of (for example) the 'academic' Radical Right. In the Radical Right books, articles, or pamphlets listed here (notes 5-13) none attack anti-sexism as overtly or as strongly as their visceral attacks on 'Marxist-egalitarianism, anti-racism, or anti-heterosexism'. One chapter in O'Keefe's earlier book (1986), does so. The contrast with radical right wing newspapers such as the ***Sun***, the ***Daily Mail***, the ***Mail on Sunday*** is very strong. In those, explicit anti-sexism is prominent.

10. Shaw (1987); Sexton (1987); O'Hear (1988).

11. The Hillgate Group (1986, 1987); O'Keefe (1990a).

12. O'Hear (1988); Trend (1988).

13. Sexton (1987); Lawlor (1990a, 1990b); O'Hear (1991).

14. CATE, the Committee for the Accreditation of Teacher Education, issued reports in 1984 and 1989. These quotes are from DES, (1989a). This report was substantially

unaltered as Circular 24/29 (DES, 1989b). The NCC document is NCC (1991) and its first three paragraphs are that:

1.1 The National Curriculum is now an important element in all initial teaching training (ITT) and most in-service education and training (INSET). Its introduction has provided a framework within which students, teachers, Higher Education (HE) tutors and Local Education Authority (LEA) staff can work together and has helped to promote a common language for professional discussion about teaching and learning.

1.2 The need to prepare new teachers for the National Curriculum has also helped to clarify thinking about what it is reasonable to expect of an ITT course. Initial training is the first stage in a process of continuing professional development through induction and subsequent INSET. No initial training programme can equip new teachers with all the knowledge, understanding and skills which they will need in their career.

1.3 During their initial training, student, articled and licensed teachers should, as an essential part of their wider professional training, develop the following knowledge, understanding and skills:

awareness of the statutory framework in which the National Curriculum functions
knowledge of subject content and teaching methods
skills in assessment, recording and reporting achievement
a view of the whole curriculum
understanding of curriculum continuity
IT capability
skills in curriculum planning and review (NCC, 1991 p.3)

15. David Hargreaves' views have been set out in a series of articles in the Times Educational Supplement. See Hargreaves (1989a, 1989b, 1989c, 1989d, 1990a, 1990b). Mary Warnock's views are set out in Warnock (1985, 1988).

16. The British Educational Research Association (BERA) research group on teacher education includes Jack Whitehead, David Hustler, John Elliot, Jean Rudduck, and Dave Hill. The UCET group (Universities Council for the Education of Teachers) embraces a wide number of University teacher educators. The 'Future of Teacher Training Group' is open to teacher educators across the binary (University/ Polytechnic and College) divide, and the 'Imaginative Projects Group' publication is just published (Hextall et al., 1991). As well the writers (Ian Hextall, Martin Lawn, Ian Menter, Susan Sidgwick and Steven Walker), this involved initially, though not finally, Colin Lacey, Dave Hill and Geoff Whitty. Organised resistance to current attacks on theory based and on college-based education has become evident in 1990 and 1991. See for example Appendix 1, the UCET 1990 press release on teacher education.

As organisations BERA and UCET do not have a specific political orientation, and are more heterogeneous than the other two specific issue groups mentioned here. In general, however, the teacher education papers at the 1989 and 1990 BERA Conferences were highly critical of Radical Right developments in ITE, and very supportive of the reflective practitioner model. The UCET press statement is

similarly caustic about (two of) the Radical Right attacks on 'teacher training'.
17. See Rosaen, Roth and Lanier (1990) and Liston and Zeichman (1987a) for details/ definition of these three conceptually distinct 'areas' of reflection. They are also developed below. The Imaginative Projects principle is referred to on p.23 of Hextall et al. (1991).
18. McIntyre (1990b). Many members of both the Rudduck/Bridges 'the Future of Teacher Training Writing Group' and the Lawn/Hextall 'Imaginative Projects' such as Jean Rudduck and Ian Menter have substantial publications and pedigrees in critiquing the Radical Right on education and teacher education. See for example Rudduck (1989, 1990) and Menter (1988), Menter and Pollard (1989) and Crozier, Menter and Pollard (1990).
19. See Ball (1990); Davies, Holland, and Minhas (1990); and Hill (1989a, 1990a). The Socialist Movement discussed Teacher Education at its Socialist Movement Education Group Conference *Education after the Tories* on 11 May 1991. Teacher educators such as Meg Maguire and Richard Hatcher set out Radical Left analyses of schooling education and teacher education. Some of the points below concerning some differences between the Radical Left and the Left in the Centre derive from Hatcher (1991).
20. Rosaen, Roth, Lanier (1990a) and Liston and Zeichner (1987a).
21. For example Clift (1988); Charvoz and Crow (1988); Shaker and Ullrich (1988).
22. For example Laboskey (1988); Zeichner (in press).
23. For example Liston and Zeichner (1987).
24. Rosaen et al. (1990).
25. Canning (1990); Rudduck and Wellington (1989)
26. Cole, Clay, and Hill (1991) and McIntyre (1990b).
27. Cole (1990).
28. Troyna and Sikes (1990)
29. Troyna and Sikes (1990).
30. Idem.
31. Idem.
32. Hill (1989a, 1989b, 1989c, 1990a, 1990b, 1990c, 1990d).
33. Such critique draws to some extent, on Zeichner (op. cit. and other works), but in particular on Giroux. Liston and Zeichner (1987) has some differences with Giroux and McLaren's view of teachers as 'transformative intellectuals'. While accepting most of their analysis Liston and Zeichner suggest that "in (Giroux and McLaren's) attempt to 'politicise' schooling we feel they blur an essential distinction between the teacher as educator and the teacher as political activist". However, together with Ira Shor (1986), Liston and Zeichner accept many dimensions of what Shor has called "egalitarian teacher education" which would include dialogic teaching, cross-cultural communication, critical literacy (Liston and Zeichner p.127). And Liston and Zeichner accept many aspects of Giroux and McLaren's passionately and vibrantly argued "conceptual apparatus for thinking about teacher education as a democratizing and counter-hegemonic force and teachers as transformative intellectuals". (In their article Liston and Zeichner detail a radical agenda for teacher education, as they do in Liston and Zeichner (1987) They also

discuss this agenda in Liston and Zeichner (1990).
A 'Transformative Intellectual' is 'one who exercises forms of intellectual and pedagogical practice which attempt to insert teaching and learning directly into the political sphere by arguing that schooling represents both a struggle for meaning and a struggle over power relations. Teachers who assume the role of transformative intellectuals treat students as critical agents, question how knowledge is produced and distributed, utilize dialogue, and make knowledge meaningful, critical, and ultimately emancipatory'. (From Giroux and McLaren (1987)).
The concepts, of cultural contestation, of the transformatory power of education are developed in Giroux (1983, 1989a, 1989b); Aranowitz and Giroux (1986); Giroux and Simon (1988); Liston and Zeichner (1987); Beyer and Zeichner (1987); Giroux and McLaren (1987, 1989b); Sarup (1986,1982); Cole (1988); Fernandes (1989a, 1989b, 1990). A fascinating example and analysis of an attempt to transform an education system in accordance with some of these perspectives is contained in Stoer (1986). Stoer discusses the left-wing Revolutionary period in Portugal from 1974 until the first Constitutional Government of 1976 and its socialist reforms such as democratic management of schools (the election of headteachers by school staffs - with candidates frequently running on party political platforms), the 'Cultural Dynamisation Campaign of the MFA (the left-wing 'Armed Forces Movement' that carried out the Revolution of April 1974).
34. See for example Wragg (1990a, 1990b); Montgomery (1989); Newsam (1990); Rudduck and Wellington (1989); Craft (1990); Adams and Tulasiewicz (1989); Baker, THES (1990); and TES (1990b).
In Craft's words 'training efficient technicians is a very worthwhile activity, but this is neither the role of teacher education, nor the requirement of the nation' (Craft 1990, p.77).
Ted Wragg often writes hilariously. See his 'Join the Right and ring the changes' in the *TES*, 6th July, 1990, p.104, on the national curriculum, teacher training, and right-wing pressure groups. See also Wragg's *None so blind as them that won't look* (1991) He attacks "ill informed and vitriolic attack on teacher training by those right-wing critics of education who show the greatest reluctance to go and look at the actual schools they criticise so readily." Wragg continues,

> " one fantasy put out is that the need for training actually prevents good people from being recruited. Yet when maths and science graduates were allowed straight into schools without training in the 1970s and 1980s, more than 2000 a year, many with higher degrees and good first degrees chose to take a PGCE course and only a hundred or so entered untrained. Another is that training does nothing for people; that little knowledge is needed to teach in a primary school, and that graduates with a decent knowledge of their subject can simply go into a classroom and start teaching. I have never been able to understand this contempt for training. I always fancy putting some hapless Nobel prizewinner in with 4D on a wet Friday afternoon to test this 'you only need to know your subject' view".
>
> "Some right-wingers seek to counter by arguing that a Nobel prizewinner in education would not be able to cope with 4D either. This is based on another

false assumption that 'education' is abstruse theory. 'Education is intelligent action informed by analysis and reflection. Nobel prizewinners, therefore, ought to be well-informed and thoughtful practitioners, still experimenting and well able to teach a variety of classes" (Wragg, 1991).

The current debate over initial teacher education is summarised in a three page article in the *TES*, pp.12-14, 7th December 1990

35. Lawlor (1990a, 1990b); O'Keefe (1990a, 1990b).

36. See for example, Wragg (1990b), MacKintyre (1990b) and Rudduck (1990) and UCET (1991). See Bates (1991) and *Teacher's Weekly* (1991) for press reaction to and summaries of the UCET press statement. Bates quotes Professor Tony Becher of Sussex University: "The Tory party has become dominated by the raving right. Some of the things they are saying are complete falsehoods." Edgar Jenkins of Leeds University said: "We are facing a complete disaster which would make the poll tax look like a fairy tale.

"If schools are given complete responsibility for training teachers without adequate resources or the desire to train them, the cumulative effect would be on that scale."

37. See Crozier, Menter, and Pollard; Wilkin; and Wragg in Booth, Furlong and Wilkin (1990), and Cowens (1990).

38. HMI (1987), *'The New Teacher in School. A Survey by H.M. Inspectors in England and Wales'*, 1987, London, HMSO.

39. CATE (1984).

40. Hazel Waddup is an East Sussex Primary school Headteacher and one of an advisory seminar group on Teacher Education advising the Labour Front Bench education team in 1990-91. Similar research has just been published by Blake and Blake (1990).

41. This research consisted of soliciting forty teachers' opinions on 'what do schools want from new teachers fresh out of their initial teacher education courses'? the research used unprompted verbal (interview) and written questionnaire questions. The fourteen statements recorded were the most common responses.

42. See Hill (1990c). The particular papers referred to here are: Smith (1990); Wale and Irons (1990); Parker (1990).

43. Wale and Irons (1990).

44. Parker (1990).

45. McLennan and Seadon (1988)

46. Rosaen, Roth, and Lanier (1990) and Canning (1990).

47. Labour Party (1989).

48. Labour Party (1990). This repeats and summarises a number of the points made in the 1989 'Children First'.

49. Idem

50. See notes 21, 22, 24, 25, and 42.

51. See Craft (1990). "Participation in regular in-service training is now expected of all teachers ... school focused and often school-based training offers enrichment - but sometimes at the cost of neglecting important national, non-local issues. All those shorter courses can and do sharpen specific skills and insights, but will this be at the expense of an understanding of the deeper processes of mind and human

interaction?" p.76.

52. See Maclennan and Seadon (1988); Hill (1989a, 1990a). The *TES* (1990a) summarises a survey of around 200 teachers who regularly supervise PGCE students from the London University Institute of Education, and a survey of 53 PGCE students. 35 of the students said they would have missed sharing the ideas and experiences with other students, and 32 said they would have missed the support of skilled tutors, if their training had consisted exclusively of classroom experience. Three out of four of the school teachers said they do not feel capable of taking responsibility for the students training. Only one in five claimed to give the student any basic ideas for lessons or detailed lesson plans.

53. See Hextall et al. (1991) pp 23-24 and HMI (1990). Taylor (1990) makes similar points about the lack of integration between ITT, Induction and INSET, as does McIntyre (1990c).

54. See Leigh (1990).

55. Labour Party (1989) op. cit., p.30.

56. Maclennan and Seadon (1988).

57. Labour Party op. cit., p.31.

58. In a series of interviews with articled teachers, mentors, and professional tutors (mentor-trainers) in Summer and Autumn 1990. This investigation, it is important to note, was carried out during and at the end of the first term of the two year course. As such the evaluation is essentially formative and not summative.

59. For example the Sussex University PGCE course pays teacher supervisors, the Crawley B.Ed. is to offer certification for 'teacher-co-operators'. A number of IT-INSET (Initial Training - In-Service Education for Teachers) schemes offer professional development and time off school into college for IT-INSET teachers. IT-INSET combines student training with In-Service training for the teachers. It is a form of classroom-based training which is deliberately reflective and evaluative, and is at present carried out, in one form or another, by thirty teacher training institutions in England and Wales. For IT-INSET in Australia see a brief article by Marks and Peacock (1988). The latest update on twenty six teacher education institutions with established IT-INSET programmes describing its operation is that by University of Leicester School of Education, Centre for Evaluation and Development in Teacher Education (1989) 'Doing IT-INSET update 1988-89' (Leicester: CEDTE). The latest book on IT-INSET, describing and evaluating it, is Everton and Impey (1989).

60. See Hill (1990c); Parker (1990); and Smith (1990a, 1990b). See also McIntyre (1990c).

61. Labour Party (1989) p.31, op. cit.

62. One notable example is the PGCE at Thames Polytechnic which is described both in Cole (1990), and in Cole, Clay and Hill (1991).

63. In note 21, 22 and 42.

64. Labour Party, (1989), op. cit., p.32.

65. Idem., p.33.

66. Idem., p.33.

67. One example is the 2-year B.Ed. for teachers with foreign qualifications (in fact mainly Indian) to achieve Qualified Teacher Status (QTS) in Britain at South Bank

Polytechnic, London. The South Bank Polytechnic also has one of a very few part-time B.Ed. degrees in the country taking five years to complete.

68. See Novoa (1990). A major problem with shortened (e.g. 2 year) B.Ed courses would be the difficulty of providing adequate preparation for teaching the National Curriculum, a point made by Sir Bill Taylor, Chair of CATE (Taylor 1990), and by many others. So, in addition to problems with European recognition, such graduates might also have problems meeting the 1991 NCC and 1989 CATE criteria and objectives for ITE courses.

69. See Maclennan and Seadon (1988) and Hill (1989a).

70. The PCFC is the Polytechnics and Colleges Funding Council.

71. See *THES* (1991a) 15 March.

72. See Taylor (1990).

Bibliography

Adams, A. and Tulasiewicz, W. (1989) Which Way the PGCE? *Times Educational Supplement*, 13th October.

Apple, M. (1989a) Critical Introduction: Ideology and the State in Educational Policy, in Dale, R. *The State and Education Policy'* Milton Keynes: Open University Press.

Apple, M. (1989b) How Equality has been Redefined in the Conservative Restoration, in Secada, W. *Equity in Education* London: Falmer Press.

Aranowitz, S. and Giroux, H. (1986) *Education under Seige: The Conservative, Liberal and Radical Debate over Schooling* London: RKP.

Ball, S. (1990) *Markets, Morality and Equality in Education* Hillcole Paper No. 5. London: the Tufnell Press.

Baker, R. (1989) PGCE courses show up faults of articled scheme. Letter to *Times Educational Supplement*, 28th July.

Banks, S. & Necco, E.(1986) Alternative Certification, Educational Training, and Job Longevity. *Action in Teacher Education* (2) 67-73 (referred to in Smith, J. 1990b)

Bartell, C. (1990) *The Support Component of the California New Teacher Project.* Paper presented at the Annual Meeting of the American Educational Research Association, 1990, Boston, Mass.

Bassey, M. (1991) All right in theory, but short on time. TES, 29 March.

Bates, S. (1991a) Clarke puts blame on Labour for 'Aiding trendy teaching' *Guardian*, 13 June.

Bates, S. (1991b) Tutors defend graduate training. *The Guardian*, 12 April.

Beyer, L. and Zeichner, K. (1987) Teacher Education in Cultural Context: Beyond Reproduction in Popkewitz, T. (ed.) *Critical Studies in Teacher Education* London: Falmer Press.

Blake, M. and Blake, D. (1990) The Teacher Training Debate: some parallels from health and social work. *Journal of Education Policy* Vol 5. No 4.

Bocock, J. (1991) Quality Teacher Education: Reflections on a Decade. *Assessment and Evaluation in Teacher Education*, Vol 16, No. 1.

Booth, M., Furlong, J., and Wilkin, M. (1990) *Partnership in Initial Teacher Training* London: Cassell.

Boyson, R. (1990) Teachers should be trained on the job and not in ivory towers. *Observer* 25th February.

Brinlee, P. R. L. and Wagner, L. (1990) *Overview of the Assessment Component of the California New Teacher Project.* Paper presented to the Annual Meeting of the American Educational Research Association, 1990, Boston, Mass.

Canning, C. (1990) *Reflection : Out on a Limb. An Intrapersonal Process and the Development of Voice.* Paper presented to the Annual Meeting of the American Educational, Research Association, 1990, Boston, Mass.

Carlson, D. (1990) *Of Basic Skills Curricula Restructuring and Crisis Tendencies in American Education.* Paper presented to the Annual Meeting of the American Education Research Association, 1990, Boston, Mass.

Carlson, D. (1987) Reproductive Theory to the Crisis of Schooling, *Harvard Educational Review*, Vol. 57, No. 3.

Carlson, D. (1988) Teachers as Political Actors: Beyond the Reproductive Theory of Teaching, in Cole, M. (ed.) *Bowles and Gintis Revisited: Correspondence and Contradiction in Educational Theory*. Lewes: Falmer Press.

CEDTE (Centre for 'Doing IT-INSET, update 1988-89')(1989). CEDTE, Leicester. Evaluation and Development in *Teacher Education*, Leicester University).

Charvoz, A. and Crow, N. (1988) *A Case Study of Journal Writing - Is it a useful tool for enhancing reflection in pre-service teachers?* Paper presented to the Annual Meeting of the American Educational Research Association, 1988, New Orleans (referred to in Rosean. et al., 1990).

Chitty, C. (1989) *Towards a New Education System: The Victory of the New Right.* London: Falmer Press.

Clay, J., Cole, M., and Hill, D. (1990) Black Achievement in Initial Teacher Education - How do we proceed into the 1990's, *Multicultural Teaching* Vol. 8 No. 3, Summer 1990.

Clift, R. T. (1988) *Learning to teach English - Maybe.* Paper presented to the Annual Meeting of the American Educational Research Association, 1988, New Orleans, (referred to in Rosean et al. 1990).

Cole, M. (1988) *Bowles and Gintis Revisited: Correspondence and Contradiction in Educational Theory*. London: Falmer Press.

Cole, M. (1990a) *Race, Class and Gender in British School Curriculum.* Paper presented at the Annual Meeting of the American Educational Research Association, 1990, Boston, Mass.

Cole, M. (1990b) *Education for Equality: Some Guidelines for Good Practice.* London: Routledge.

Cole, M., Clay, J., and Hill, D. (1991) The Citizen as 'individual' and nationalist or as 'social' and internationalist? What is the role of education? *Critical Social Policy,* Vol. 10, No 3.

Cowens, R., (1990) Teacher Education: A Comparative View, in Graves, N. *Initial Teacher Education: Policies and Progress*. London: Institute of Education, University of London.

Craft, M. (1990) Charting the Changes in Teacher Education, *Cambridge Journal of Education,* Vol 20 No. 1.

Crozier, G., Menter, I., and Pollard, A. (1990) Changing Partnership in Booth, M., Furlong, J., and Wilkin, M. *Partnership in Initial Teacher Training.* London: Cassell

Culloden School (1991) *Culloden: The real story,* Culloden Story, 4 Blair Street, London E14 0NW, March.

Dale, R. (1989) *The State and Education Policy.* Milton Keynes: Open University Press.

Darling-Hammond, L., Hudson, L. and Kirby, S. (1989) *Redesigning Teacher Education. Opening the Door for New Recruits to Science and Mathematics Teaching.* Santa Monica, CA : The Rand Corporation (referred to in Smith, J. 1990b).

Davies, A., Holland, J. & Minhas, R. (1990) *Equal Opportunities in the new ERA*. Hillcole Paper No. 2, London: the Tufnell Press.

Denton, J. and Smith, N. (1988) *A Cost Effectiveness Evaluation of Alternate Secondary Level Teacher Preparation Programs*, Paper presented at the Annual Meeting of the American Educational Research Association, 1988, New Orleans. (referred to in Smith, J. 1990).

DES (Department of Education and Science) (1984) *Initial Teacher Training: Approval of Courses* (Circular 3/84) London: DES.

DES (1989a) *The Education (Teachers) Regulations 1989*. Circular 18/89 (on Licensed Teachers) London: HMSO.

DES (1989b) *The Provisional Teacher Program in New Jersey* - a paper by Her Majesty's Inspectorate. London: HMSO.

DES (1989c) *Future Arrangements for the Accreditation of course of Initial Teacher Training*, A Consultation Document'. London: HMSO.

DES (1989d) *Initial Teacher Training: Approval of Courses*. Circular 24/89'. London: HMSO.

DES (1989e) *Articled Teacher Pilot Scheme: Invitation to Bid for Funding*. London: DES 27th June 1989.

DES. (1989f) DES Press Release, *New 'on the job' teacher training scheme for graduates*, 27th June. London: DES.

DES. (1989g) *TASC* (Teaching as a Second Career) pamphlet on the Articled Teacher Scheme, 1st edition. November 1989. London: DES

DES (1990) *Teacher Training a Priority Area*, Press Release, 385/90, November, London: HMSO.

Everton, T. and Impey, G. *IT-INSET Partnership in Training - The Leicestershire Experience*. London: David Fulton.

Fernandes J. V. (1988) From the Theories of Social and Cultural Reproduction to the Theory of Resistance. *British Journal of Sociology of Education*, Vol 9 No 2, 1988.

Fernandes J. V. (1989) *The Sociology of Education in Teacher Training Curricula*. Paper presented at the 12th International Sociology of Education Conference, Birmingham, England.

Fernandes J. V. (1990) *Reflexoes(as) Sobre o Ensino da Sociologia da Educacao na Formacao de Professores*, 1st International Sociology of Education Conference, Faro: Portugal.

Giroux, H. (1983) *Theory and Resistance in Education: A Pedagogy for the Opposition*. London: Heinemann.

Giroux, H. (1989a) *Teachers as Intellectuals: Towards a Critical Pedagogy of Learning*. Massachusetts: Bergin and Garvey.

Giroux, H. and McLaren, P. (1987) *Teacher Education as a Counter-Public Sphere: Notes Towards a Redefinition* in Popkewitz, T., op. cit.

Giroux, H. and McLaren, P. (1989a) Teacher Education and the Politics of Engagement: and The Case for Democratic Schooling. *Harvard Education Review*, Vol 56, No 3.

Giroux, H. and McLaren, P. (eds.) (1989b) *Critical Pedagogy, the State and Cultural Struggle*. New York: State University of New York Press.

Giroux, H. and Simon, R. (1988) Schooling, Popular Culture and a Pedagogy of Possibility. *Boston University Journal of Education*, Vol. 170, No. 1.

Gordon, A. (1991) Brave new breed learn their schoolroom skills on the job, *The Mail on Sunday*, 5 May.

Gray, D. and Lynn, D. (1988) *New Teacher, Better Teachers: A Report of Two Initiatives in New Jersey. Council for Basic Education*, Washington, D. C. p.8. (referred to in Smith, J. 1990b)

Graves, N. J. (ed.) (1990) *Initial Teacher Education : Policies and Progress*. London: Institute of Education, University of London.

Guardian, (1991) What trainee teachers really need to be taught (Letters page) 2nd April.

Guyton, E. (1990) *The Mentor Component of the 1988-89 Georgia Alternative Certification Program*. Paper Presented at the Annual Meeting of the American Educational Research Association, 1990, Boston, Mass.

Hargreaves, D. (1989a) Judge radicals by results. *TES*, 6th October. London.

Hargreaves, D. (1989b) Out of B.Ed. and into Practice. *TES*, 8th September. London.

Hargreaves, D. (1989c) PGCE assessment fails the test. *TES*, 3rd November. London.

Hargreaves, D. (1989d) Looking at a model of health. *TES*, 1st December. London.

Hargreaves, D. (1989e) Merit and Market. *TES*. 14th April. London.

Hargreaves, D. (1990a) *Another Radical Approach to the Reform of initial teacher training*, Paper delivered at UCET conference, 1990.

Hargreaves, D. (1990b) Remission on a Life Sentence: Flexibility is the key to Teacher Training. *THES*. 21st September, London.

Hatcher, R. (1991) *Labour's education policy*. Paper given to the Social Movement Education Group Conference *Education after the Tories* London, 11 May.

Hessari, R. and Hill, D. (1989) *Practical Approaches to Multi-Cultural Learning and Teaching in the Primary Classroom*. London: Routledge.

Hextall, I., Lawn, M., Menter, I., Sidgwick, S., and Walker, S. (1991) *Imaginative Projects: Arguments for a new teacher education*, London, Goldsmiths' College, University of London.

Hill, D. (1989a) *Charge of the Right Brigade: the Radical Right's attack on Teacher Education*. Brighton: The Hillcole Group/Institute for Education Policy Studies.

Hill, D. (1989b) Teacher Education, teachers and the attack on equality. *NUT Education Review*, Autumn 1989, Vol 73 No 2.

Hill, D. (1989c) Resisting the Radical Right's Assault on Teacher Education. *Liberal Education/General Educator*. Winter 1989.

Hill, D. (1990a) *Something Old, Something New, Something Borrowed, Something Blue: Teacher Education, Schooling and the Radical Right in Britain and the USA*. Hillcole Paper No. 3, London: Tufnell Press.

Hill, D. (1990b) *Thatcherism and the Attack on the Teacher Education Curriculum in Britain*. Paper presented to the Annual Meeting of the American Educational Research 1990, Boston, Mass.

Hill, D. (1990c) *Initial Teacher Education and the Development of Transformative Intellectuals*. Paper presented to the Annual Meeting of the British Educational Research Association, Roehampton, London.

Hill, D. (1990d) *Proposals for the Future Organisation of Teacher Education in England and Wales: Schools as Clients and their Relationships with Teacher Training/Education Institutions*. Paper presented to Teacher Education subcommittee of the NUT (National Union of Teachers), and also to the Teacher Education Subcommittee of NATFHE (National Association of Teachers in Further and Higher Education), both in London.

Hill, Dave (1991a) The Hillcole Group, *Forum*, Spring, Vol 33, No 2.

Hillcole Group (in press 1991) *Changing the future: Redprint for Education*. London: the Tufnell Press.

Hillgate Group (1986) *Whose Schools? A Radical Manifesto*. London: Hillgate.

Hillgate Group (1987) *The Reform of British Education - From Principles to Practice*. London: The Claridge Press.

Hillgate Group (1989) *Learning to Teach*. London: The Claridge Press.

HMI (1988) *The New Teacher in School* - A Survey by HM Inspectors in England and Wales 1987. London: HMSO.

HMI (1990) *Perspectives on teacher education: Other trainers' views*. London: HMSO.

HMI (1991a) *Culloden Primary School: A Report by HMI*, reference 101/91 (published 16 April 1991). London: HMSO.

HMI (1991b) *Standards in education*, London: HMSO.

Howey, K. R. (1985) Six Major Functions of Staff Development, An Expanded Initiative, *Journal of Teacher Education*, Vol 36, No 1. (referred to in Wagner et al., 1990).

Huling-Austin, L. (1986) Factors to be Considered in Alternative Certification Programs: What can be Learned from Teacher Induction Research? *Action in Teacher Education* 8 (2) 51-57 (referred to in Smith, J. 1990b).

James, C. (1991) *Records of Experience of Students taking a Concurrent Degree and Certificate in Education Course*. Paper presented to the Bath University Conference *Conceptualising Reflection in Teacher Development* Bath University, March.

Jones, K. (1989) *Right Turn - the Conservative Revolution in Education?* London: Hutchinson.

Knight, C. (1990) *The Making of Tory Education Policy in Post-War Britain 1950-1986*. London: Falmer Press.

Labour Party (1989) *Children First: Labour's Policy for Raising Standards in Schools*. London: Labour Party.

Labour Party (1990) *Aiming High: Raising Standards in Britain's Schools*. London: The Labour Party.

Laboskey, V. (1988) *Schon into the practice of teaching: Proceed with caution*. Paper presented at the Annual Meeting of the American Educational Research Association, 1988, New Orleans. (referred to by Rosaen, et al., 1990).

Lawlor, S. (1990a) *Teachers Mistaught: Training in theories or education in subjects?* London: Centre for Policy Studies.

Lawlor, S. (1990b) Something is Wrong in the Classroom, *Daily Telegraph* 11th June.

Leigh, S. (1990) *Building the Bridge: Profiling the student teacher. A new approach to assessment.* Lancaster: Lancaster University School of Education.

Lightfoot, L. (1991a) School that fails its children, *The Mail on Sunday*, 3 March.

Lightfoot, L. (1991b) Clarke orders probe at Culloden, *The Mail on Sunday*, 10 March.

Liston, D. P. and Zeicher, K. M. (1987) Reflective Teacher Education and Moral Deliberation. *Journal of Teacher Education* Nov.-Dec. 1987 pp 2-8. (referred to by Rosaen et al., 1990).

Liston, D. P. and Zeicher, K. M. (1987) Critical Pedagogy and Teacher Education, *Journal of Education*, (Boston) Vol 169, No 3.

Liston, D. and Zeicher, K. (1990) Reflective Teaching and Action Research in Preservice Teacher Education. *Journal of Education for Teaching*, Vol 16, No. 3.

Little, J. W. (1990) Presentation to the California New Teacher Project Directors, as a report of Work in Progress, to be included in the AERA Fourth Hand book of Research on Teaching (forthcoming) (referred to in Wagner et al., 1990).

Lodge, B. (1991a) Trainers braced for shunt into classroom, *TES*, 29 March.

Lodge B. (1991b) Licensing laws to be relaxed, *TES*, 12 April.

Lutz, F. and Hutton, J. (1989) Alternative Teacher Certification: Its Policy Implications for Classroom Personnel Practice, *Education Evaluation and Policy Analysis*, 11 (3) 237-254 (referred to by Smith, J. 1990b).

MacLeod, D. (1991) Fallon's support crucial to success of campaign, *The Independent*, 18 March.

Maguire, M. (1991) *Teacher Education.* Paper given to the Socialist Movement Education Group Conference, *Education after the Tories*, London, 11 May.

Marks, M. and Peacock, A. (1988) Teacher Education in a Collaborative Context: Piloting IT-INSET in Australia. *The South Pacific Journal of Teacher Education*, Vol. 16, No 2.

Massey, R. (1991a) Minister wades into school trendies, *Daily Mail*, 13 June.

Massey, R. (1991b) Stand up to trendies: Teachers must fight theories harming pupils, says Minister, *Daily Mail*, 21 March.

Massey, R. (1991c) Forget the theory, just teach us to teach, *Daily Mail*, 30 April.

McIntyre, D. (1990a) The Oxford Internship Scheme and the Cambridge Analytical Framework: Models of Partnership in Initial Teacher Education, in Booth, M. Furlong, J. and Wilkins, M. *Partnership in Initial Teacher Training.* London: Cassell.

McIntyre, D. (1990b) Ideas and Principles Guiding the Internship Scheme, Paper delivered at UCET Conference, London, 1990.

McIntyre, D. (1990c) 'The efficient use of human resolves in teacher education'. Paper delivered to the SCETT Annual Residential Conference, November 1990, *Teacher Education Policies for the 1990s.* Reported in SCETT (1991).

McLennan, S. and Seadon, T. (1988) What Price School - Based Work. Reflections on a School - Sited PGCE Method Course. *Cambridge Journal of Education*, Vol 18, No 3.

Menter, I. (1988) Teaching Practise stasis: Racism, sexism and school experience in initial teacher education, in Terrell, C., and Coles, D., (eds.) *Recent Innovations in Initial Teacher Education for Intending Primary School Teachers*. Cheltenham: College of St. Paul and St. Mary.

Menter, I. and Pollard, A. (1989) The Implications of the National Curriculum for reflective practice in initial teacher education. *Westminster Studies in Education*, Vol 12.

Montgomery, D. (1989) Teaching skills can so often outweigh subject specialism, Letter to *TES*, 6th December.

Nash, M. (1990) Teacher Education Today, in Graves, N. J. (ed.) *Initial Teacher Education: Policies and Progress*. London: Institute of Education, University of London.

National Curriculum Council (1991) *The National Curriculum and the Initial Training of Student, Articled and Licensed Teachers*, York: National Curriculum Council.

Newsam, P. (1989) Ready for the Road *TES*, 22nd September.

Novoa, A. (in press) Six Countries Study of Reform Practices: An outline of the problem in Teacher Education, The Case of Portugal.

O'Hear, A. (1988) *Who Teaches the Teachers? A Contribution to Public Debate.* London: Social Affairs Unit.

O'Hear, A. (1990) Not dreamt of in Dewey's philosophy. *TES* 6th April.

O'Hear, A. (1991) Getting the teachers we deserve, *The Guardian*, 19 March.

O'Keefe, D. (1986) *The Wayward Curriculum: A Cause for Parents Concern London*: Social Affairs Unit.

O'Keefe, D. (1990a) *The Wayward Elite*. London: the Adam Smith Institute.

O'Keefe, D. (1990b) The Real Lesson to be Learned in our Schools, *Daily Mail*, 9th March.

O'Keefe, D. (1990c) Equality and Childhood: Education and the Myths of Teacher Training, in Graves, N. J. (ed.) *Initial Teacher Education, Policies and Progress*, London: Institute of Education, University of London.

Parker, M. (1990) Adolescent Dancing and the Mentoring of Beginning Teachers. Paper presented at the American Education Research Association Annual Meeting, Boston, April 1990.

Popkewitz, T. (ed.) (1987) *Critical Studies in Teacher Education*. London: Falmer Press.

Richardson, R. (1991) HM Inconsiderate: The recent inspection of Culloden Primary School was a sorry affair, *TES*, 26 April.

Rosean, C. Roth, K., & Lanier, P. (1990) Becoming a Reflective Teacher of Subject Matter. Paper prepared for the Annual Meeting of the American Educational Research Association, Boston, Massachusetts, April 1990.

Rudduck, J. (1989) Doing it is not enough. *The Guardian*, 7th February.

Rudduck, J. and Wellington, J. (1989) Encouraging the spirit of enquiry in initial teacher training. *Forum*(for the discussion of new trends in education), Vol 31, No. 2.

Rudduck, J. (1990) UDEs for the 1990s : The distinctive contribution of Higher Education in the partnership of initial teacher education. Paper delivered at UCET conference 1990.

Sarup, M. (1982) *Education, State and Crisis, A Marxist Perspective.* London: RKP.

Sarup, M. (1986) *The Politics of Multi-Racial Education.* London: Routledge.

SCETT (Standing Committee for the Education and Training of Teachers in the Public Sector) (1991) SCETT News No. 19, February, 1991.

Secada, W. (ed.) (1989) *Equity in Education.* Lewes: Falmer Press.

Sexton, S. (1987) *Our Schools - A Radical Policy.* London: Institute for Economic Affairs.

Shaker, P. and Ullrich, W. (1988) An educational psychology curriculum designed to foster reflective thinking. Paper presented at the Annual Meeting of the American Educational Research Association, New Orleans, (referred to in Rosean et al., 1990).

Shaw, B. (1987) Teacher Training: The Misdirection of British teaching in O'Keefe, D., *The Wayward Curriculum.* London: Social Affairs Unit.

Schon, D. (1983) *The Reflective Practitioner.* New York: Basic Books.

Schon, D. (1987) *Educating the Reflective Practitioner.* London: Jossey Bass.

Scruton, R. (1990) Labour's great education fraud. *The Sunday Telegraph*, 9th December.

Shor, I. (1986) Culture Wars.

Silva, L. (1990) E Preciso Restaurar o Prestigio da Professao Docente. *O Professor*, Maio 1990, No 5 (3a. Serie)

Smith, J. M. (1990a) School Districts as Teacher Training Institutions in the New Jersey Alternative Route Program, Clearwater, Florida, Eastern Educational Research Association (referred to in Smith, J. 1990b).

Smith, J. M. (1990b) A Comparative Study of the State Regulations for the Operation of the New Jersey Provisional Teacher Certification Program. Paper presented to the Annual Conference of the American Education Research Association, 1990, Boston, Mass.

Stoer, S. R. (1986) *Educaco e Mudanca Social em Portugal 1970-1980, Uma Decada de Transicao.* Porto, Portugal: Edicoes Afrontamento.

Stoer, S. R., Stoleroff, A. D., and Correia, J. A. (1990) O Novo Vocacionalismo na Politica Educativa em Portugal e a Reconstrucao da Logica da Acumulacao Coimbra, Portugal: *Revista Critica de ciencias Sociais* 29 Fevereiro 1990.

Straw, J. (1989) *Straw Proposes Eight Point Plan on Teacher Shortages.* Press Release, House of Commons, 7th November.

Swanwick, K. (1990) The Necessity of Teacher Education, in Graves, N. J. *Initial Teacher Education: Policies and Progress*, London: Institute of Education, University of London.

Taylor, W. (1990) Which way now? The prospects for Teacher Education. Paper delivered to the SCETT Annual Residential Conference (November 1990). Reported in SCETT (1991).

Teachers Weekly (1991) Academics give their defence, 18 April.

Teodoro, Antonio (1990) Sobre e mal-estar na Profissao Docente e a Construcao de uma Identidade Profissional nos Professores. *O Professor*, April 1990, No 4 (3a serie) (Lisbon)

Terrell, C. and Coles, D. (eds.) *Recent Innovations in Initial Teacher Education for Intending Primary School Teachers*. Cheltenham: College of St. Paul and St. Mary.

Times Education Supplement (1989) News Focus (on the Radical Right) London: *TES* 6th October.

Times Education Supplement (1990a) Teachers not ready to fulfil training role. London: *TES*. 28th December.

Times Education Supplement (1990b) Article on teacher education pp. 12-14 and p. 6. *TES*, London, 7th December.

Times Higher Education Supplement (1990) Rights' Teaching Plans incur V-Cs wrath. *THES* 30th November.

Times Higher Education Supplement (1991c) PCFC Lifeline for the overcrowded, *THES*, 15 March.

Times Higher Education Supplement (1991a) DES woos overseas recruits, *THES*, 5 April.

Times Education Supplement (1991b) Clash on Teaching Schools, *THES*, 3 May.

Trend, M. (1988) How Teachers Learn. *The Spectator*, 15th October.

Troyna, B. and Sikes, P. (1989) Putting the why back into teacher education. *Forum* (for the discussion of new trends in education) Autumn 1989 Vol 32 No 1.

UCET (Universities Council for the Education of Teachers) (1990). Press statement on teacher education, UCET (printed as appendix).

UCET (Universities Council for the Education of Teachers) (1991). Press Conference Statement, UCET, 17 April.

Wale, W. and Irons, E. J. (1990) An Evaluative Study of Texas Alternative Certification Programs. Paper presented at the Annual Meeting of the American Educational Research Association, 1990, Boston, Mass.

Warnock, M. (1985) *Teacher Teach Thyself*. London: BBC Publications.

Warnock, M. (1988) *A Common Policy for Education*. Oxford: Oxford University Press.

West, D. (1991) Academe and common sense, UCET, 17 April.

Whitty, G. (1990) Alternative Approaches to Teacher Education. Background paper for the Labour Party House of Commons Seminar on Teacher Education, 25th July. Unpublished.

Whitty, G, Barton, L. and Pollard, A. (1987) *Ideology Control in Critical Studies in Teacher & Education*. Lewes : Falmer Press.

Wragg, T. (1988) *Education in the Market Place. The Ideology behind the 1988 Education Bill*. London: National Union of Teachers.

Wragg, T. (1990a) The Two Routes into Teaching, in Booth, M. Furlong, J. and Wilkin, M. *Partnership in Initial Teacher Training?* London: Cassell.

Wragg, T. (1990b) Stand by your B.Eds. Paper delivered at the UCET Conference, London, 1990.

Wragg, T. (1990c) Join the Right and ring the changes. *TES*. 6th July.

Wragg, T. (1991) None so blind as them that won't look, *TES*, 5 April.

Zeichner, K. and Liston, D. (1987) Teaching Student Teachers to Reflect. *Harvard Education Review*, Vol 57 No. 1 Feb. 1987.

Zeichner, K. (in press) Preparing Reflective Teachers: An overview of instructional strategies that have been employed as pre-service teacher education programs. *International Journal of Research in Teacher Education*. (referred to in Rosaen et al., 1990)

Appendix 1

Universities Council for the Education of Teachers (UCET) Press Statement on teacher training 19th June, 1990

We are very concerned at the degree of credibility given by some newspapers to ill-informed statements on teacher training made by politically motivated groups such as the Adam Smith Institute and the Centre for Policy Studies. In recent months considerable coverage has been given to what are termed 'reports' on teacher training from these political groups.

The term 'report' usually signifies a carefully considered analysis based on scrutiny of the evidence. Yet both *The Wayward Elite* by Dennis O'Keefe, published by the Adam Smith Institute and *Teachers Mistaught* by Sheila Lawlor, are personal prejudices of one individual.

These political tracts make numerous unsubstantiated assertions which have been reproduced uncritically by some newspapers. Sheila Lawlor, for example, claims that teacher training "deters good graduates from entering the profession". Yet training for graduates has been compulsory since 1973, and throughout the late 1970s and early 1980s the Government actually cut back the numbers of training places because there was thought to be an over-supply of teachers. Even after 1973, when maths and science graduates were exempted from the training requirement, the vast majority chose to take a teacher training course. Only a minority elected to enter the profession without training.

In addition it is being said that teacher training is socialist, that it imposes "the same style on all teachers, for all subjects, for all children". We refute these unfounded and unjustifiable statements with the utmost vigour. Teacher trainers themselves hold different political and philosophical views and are not dominated by any single ideology. Training courses are carefully conceived to enable teachers to see children as individuals. Courses for primary and secondary teachers, or for those specialising in mathematics, science, English or modern languages, are specially designed to recognise the differences in teaching styles which will be required for children at various ages in different contexts.

Teacher trainers are further accused by Sheila Lawlor of including in their courses topics such as special educational needs, multicultural education and equal opportunities, which she calls "a series of random topics, chosen, it appears because of their fascination for educationalists". Yet all these topics are required by the Government. The DES Circular 24/89 lays down the conditions which all training courses must meet in order to be accredited by the Secretary of State. In Section 6 it states "On completion of their courses, students and should be aware of links and common ground between subjects and be able to incorporate into their teaching cross-curricular dimensions (e.g. equal opportunities, multicultural education and personal and social education)". It also states, "On completion of their course students should have developed the capacity to identify gifted pupils and pupils with special educational needs or with learning difficulties; and to understand the

ways in which the potential of such pupils can be developed", and "Students should learn to guard against preconceptions based on race, gender, religion or other attributes of pupils and understand the need to promote equal opportunities."
Far from being 'random topics', these are actually Government requirements.
However, it should also be said that, although these matters are a Government requirement, teacher trainers are in any case strongly committed to ensuring that all children in our society have the best possible opportunities to learn, irrespective of their social background, sex or religion.
By contrast with the ill-informed and unresearched assertions of politically motivated groups such as the Adam Smith Institute and the Centre for Policy Studies, there have been proper surveys of teacher training based on visits to institutions, scrutiny of course content and methodology, visits to schools to see students on teaching practice and interviews with tutors and students. After a five year programme of lengthy visits by teams from Her Majesty's Inspectorate during the late 1980s, during which every single university teacher training course was visited, far from castigating universities, HMI commented favourably on what they had seen. They stated that universities were able to recruit well-qualified sixth formers and final year undergraduates to their bachelor degrees in education and postgraduate certificate courses; that students "nearly all show signs of becoming competent teachers and some are exceptionally able"; that "the increasing integration of educational theory with professional training and practical experience in schools not only makes effective use of the limited time available, but also enables students to relate all aspects of their course to the work in the classroom".
HMI congratulated universities for the wide range of their inservice training programmes, their links with practising teachers and also commented, "the quality of research in university departments of education has won national and international recognition and it enriches the teaching on initial training courses". HMI encouraged universities to publish the reports on individual departments of education, even though they were not obliged to, on the grounds that there was so much good practice in universities that should be made more widely known.
We deplore, therefore, the attempts by politically motivated groups to smear teaching training, to make unsubstantiated allegations, and to parade personal whim and prejudice as 'evidence' in what they claim to be a 'report'.

Appendix 2

Press release by Tim Eggar

Teacher training is an area of anxiety and concern and, if things are not right something must be done about it. The principal concern, simply, is that teacher training does not prepare teachers adequately for their work. The specific things complained about are that the training is not relevant; there is too much theory and not enough practice, and that trainers have little or no classroom experience and

peddle pet ideas, including some political bias,
Teacher Training a Priority Area. Press Notice 385/90 November

Appendix 3

Universities Council for the Education of Teachers Press release 17th April 1991

The heads of University Departments of Education declared that the campaign seeking to discredit teacher training completely misrepresented teacher training as it is conducted today. The Universities Council for the Education of Teachers welcomes any properly researched evaluation of the different ways of training teachers but regards what is now being put about as an ill-informed travesty of what goes on in teacher training today. The following points were put forward by UCET:-

1. The content of teacher training courses is controlled by the Secretary of State through the Council for the Accreditation of Teachers (CATE). Courses which do not match his criteria are not accredited but almost all have been accredited without difficulty.

2 Sound training must have a theoretical component if we are to have teachers who, like other professionals, know why they are acting as they do. We need thinking teachers able to exploit with their pupils the opportunities provided by the national curriculum and its associated assessment programme. The appropriate balance between theory, applications and practice is established in the Secretary of State's criteria.

3. The criticisms that too much time is spent on psychology and on sociology are patently false. CATE receives a full breakdown of each course before it is approved. The Secretary of State's criteria include matters which cannot be dealt with without calling in these disciplines; examples are children with learning difficulties, the education of ethnic groups, gender, etc. The point was dealt with specifically by the Senior Chief Inspector in his report Standards in Education 1989/90 (HMI/DES 1991). "Initial teacher training courses are no longer overloaded with educational theory or the history, psychology, or sociology of education."

4. All students are required to spend a period of continuous practice in schools and in addition undertake substantial amounts of school-based work as part of the process of relating theory to practice and practice to theory. The full practice is supervised by university tutors working in close collaboration with their classroom counterparts and is externally assessed. Any student who does not achieve a satisfactory standard in practical teaching fails the course.

5. UCET strongly supports school-based training; indeed it was universities which pioneered these approaches over 20 years ago. The Senior Chief Inspector (Standards in Education op. cit.) reports "So extensive are the working partnerships between colleges and schools becoming.... that the demands upon some schools are now very heavy. The tricky question of how to fund the schools... is now a pressing one." UCET agrees; the Articled Teacher Scheme (see 6) does precisely

that. For both conventional school-based training and for the Articled Teacher Scheme the UDEs are an economic way of providing the expertise and resources needed in each region for quality training.

6. UCET supports the Articled Teacher Scheme in which the graduate student is paid for certain teaching contributions and at the same time takes a two year PGCE in the local teacher training establishment. Many university departments are actively engaged in this scheme and UCET looks forward to receiving the HMI evaluation of this innovation. Meanwhile it notes that the Articled Teacher Scheme had turned out to be more expensive than conventional training, including those forms of the latter which are strongly school based.

7. UCET has strong reservations about the Licensed Teacher Scheme in which an employer hires an untrained person (who need not be a graduate) and provides on-the-job training without any formal award being made. There need be no input from nor contact with the local teacher training establishments. It is to be regretted that the people recruited to this scheme (including many of overseas origin) are not being given the opportunity to obtain the standard entry qualification to the profession. It is also quite wrong that having set up an official accrediting body (The Council for the Accreditation of Teacher Education) the Government decided that Licensed Teacher courses did not have to be submitted to that body even though all other courses of initial teacher training are required to do so.

8. An important criterion for appointment as a teacher trainer is a record of achievement as a classroom teacher. Once appointed teacher trainers return regularly to the classroom in order to develop further their special skills as teacher trainers. Courses are not accredited unless those who teach pedagogical aspects regularly practise what they teach.

9. Student teachers are often welcomed into the schools because if the up-to-date information they have learned from their tutors on developments in the national curriculum. The training institutions represent a resource centre which the schools draw upon as they cooperate in training the next generation of teachers.

10. Suggestions that teacher training could be entirely school-based show little knowledge of (i) pressures in schools today, (ii) what the process of professional formation entails. Our European partners are moving more strongly towards higher education-based training. The nursing profession in the UK has decided to abandon learn-on-the-job training. UCET values greatly the partnership with schools and wishes to see schools reimbursed for the work they do in the preparation of teachers but it insists also that to remove training from higher education would be the first step towards de-professionalisation of a profession which has had less than fair treatment from successive governments. There is no evidence that teachers, given their present loads, would wish to take on the whole of this task.

11. Teacher trainers play a key part in bringing well-qualified people into the profession. If all the training had to be done whilst in employment, the schools, especially those that had 'opted out', would each year have to compete for new graduates against the competition provided by other employers of new graduates. The implications of this for cost and management of the education service would

be considerable!
12. UCET accepts that there is always room for further improvement on teacher training/ Meanwhile the Senior Chief Inspector's Report for 1989/90 provides an authoritative summary of the current state since it is based upon observation by the corps of specialist teacher training inspectors. "The initial training of primary and secondary teachers is satisfactory or better in most institutions. In several, in both the university and public sectors, the quality is good or outstanding. Of all the work inspected, 85% was judged satisfactory or better. Most students are well-motivated and able to plan classroom work effectively, though most find it difficult to organise and provide suitable work for pupils of different abilities in the same class, and to assess and record pupils' progress. Generally, four-year BEd and one-year PGCE courses provide an appropriate balance of theory and practice." (Standards in Education op. cit.)

HILLCOLE GROUP PUBLICATIONS

No. 1 Charge of the Right Brigade: The Radical Right's Attack on Teacher Education

Dave Hill.

With its introduction of the licensed and apprenticed teacher route into school teaching and its bypassing of and proposed changing of the curriculum for teacher training, the Government, urged on by the Radical Right, is seeking to 'conform' teacher education to its own ideology. This booklet critiques such developments argues that teacher educators must persist in developing - reflexive teachers as 'transformative intellectuals', and adapt new initiatives in teacher training for this purpose.

ISBN 1 872155 00 6 *temporarily out of print*

No. 2 Equal Opportunities in the new ERA

Ann Marie Davies, Janet Holland and Rehana Minhas.

This booklet examines the implications for equal opportunities in relation to gender, race and class, of recent changes in education, focussing on the ERA and the National Curriculum. The broad political and social context in which these changes have taken place is outlined, drawing particular attention to the ideological groundwork provided by the New Right. The rhetoric of choice and parental power is related to the actual process of consultation undertaken before the legislation was introduced and during its process into law.The National Curriculum is discussed along with the equal opportunities implications of Local Management of Schools, open enrollment, testing and assessment and changes in methods and content of the curriculum. The effects of the new legislation is explored for a number of relevant groups including pupils, teachers, heads and governing bodies, parents and communities and LEAs. The book concludes with proposals for a charter of demands which would ensure equality and democracy in education.

ISBN 1 872767 00 1 **£3.95**

No. 3 Something Old, Something New, Something Borrowed, Something Blue: Schooling, Teacher Education and the Radical Right in Britain and the USA

Dave Hill.

In this booklet, Hill examines Radical Right attacks on liberal-democratic and social-egalitarian models of schooling and teacher education in Britain and the USA. He contrasts the layers of Radical Right permeation and asserts the relatively greater resistance in Britain. The booklet goes on to compare the Radical Right with respect to academia and the domination by testing and textbook and the deskilling and proletarianization of teachers in the

USA and draws out the implications for Britain. It ends with a critique of the threefold way in which the Government is seeking to 'conform' and bypass teacher education - an assault on critical reflective teaching - and calls for a partnership of teacher educators, teachers, teacher unions and local education authorities.

ISBN 1 872767 05 2 **£3.95**

No. 4 Training Turns to Enterprise: Vocational Education in the Market Place

Pat Ainley.

Ainley reviews the phases of education policy since the war to ask what has become of the penultimate 'vocational' phase from 1976 to 1987. He looks briefly at what is left of the Youth Training Scheme before concentrating on the Technical and Vocational Education Initiative and the City Technology Colleges. The latter is seen as the last fling of vocationalism and the prototype for the market model of education. He concludes by describing the review of vocational qualifications being undertaken by the National Council for Vocational Qualifications, predicting in its 'access' and modularisation the future direction of many education reforms. He argues that progressive educationalists will have to steer a difficult course between opening that which they can to genuine access for all and the spuriousness of 'enterprise'.

ISBN 872767 10 9 **£3.95**

No. 5 Markets, Morality and Equality in Education

Stephen Ball

The booklet explores the political and ideological antecedents of the *education market* established by the Education Reform Act. The operation and implications of the market for school organisation, the curriculum, teachers' work and conditions and social equality and justice are considered. The booklet argues that the education market fulfils the requirements of market forces outlined by neo-liberal economist Freidrich Hayek and sponsored by the New Right think tanks (Institute of Economic Affairs, Centre for Policy Studies, Adam Smith Institute). In this respect the ERA constitutes a fundamental social and political experiment with the lives and futures of the children of England and Wales.

ISBN 1 872767 15 X **£3.95**

the Tufnell Press
47 Dalmeny Road,
London, N7 0DY

ORDER FORM

Please send me the following:

	Price	Quantity	Total

Total amount enclosed ________

Please make cheques payable to the Tufnell Press

NAME ____________________
ADDRESS

____

____

____

W5/1990